WOMEN, COMMUNICATION,
CAREERS

DATE DUE			**DATE DUE**
NOV 3 0 '83			
DEC 3 '86			
DEC 19 '90			
APR 2 '98			
MAY 0 1 '95			
18 '9'			
NOV 2 1 '97			
DEC 1 8 '02			

Communication Research and Broadcasting No. 3

Editor:
Internationales Zentralinstitut
für das Jugend- und Bildungsfernsehen (IZI)

Women, Communication, and Careers

Edited by
Marianne Grewe-Partsch
Gertrude J. Robinson

K·G·Saur
München·NewYork·London·Paris 1980

Editor of the series:
Internationales Zentralinstitut für das Jugend- und Bildungsfernsehen

Editors of this issue:
Dr. Marianne Grewe-Partsch, Dr. Gertrude J. Robinson

Editorial assistant:
Käthe Nowacek

Address of editor and editorial staff:
Internationales Zentralinstitut für das Jugend- und Bildungsfernsehen
Rundfunkplatz 1, D-8000 München 2
Telephone (0 89) 59 00-21 40, Telex 05 29831

K. G. Saur Verlag KG
Pössenbacherstr. 2 b, POB 711009
D-8000 München 71
Federal Republic of Germany
Tel. (0 89) 79 89 01
Telex 5212067 saur d

ISBN 3-598-20202-4

CIP-Kurztitelaufnahme der Deutschen Bibliothek

Women, communication, and careers / ed. by
Marianne Grewe-Partsch ; Gertrude J. Robinson.
– München, New York, London, Paris : Saur, 1980.
   (Communication research and broadcasting ; No. 3)
   ISBN 3-598-20202-4 (München)
   ISBN 0-89664-172-4 (New York)

NE: Grewe-Partsch, Marianne [Hrsg.]

K. G. Saur Publishing, Inc.
175 Fifth Avenue
New York, NY 10010
U.S.A.
Tel. (212) 477-2500
Telex 0023/238386

ISBN 0-89664-172-4

Clive Bingley Ltd. & K. G. Saur Ltd.
1-19 New Oxford Street
London WC1A 1NE
United Kingdom
Tel. 01-404 48 18
Telex 24902 bingle g

K. G. Saur Editeur S.a.r.l.
38, rue de Bassano
F-75008 Paris
France
Tel. 7 23 55-18
Telex Iso Bur. 6 30 144

Contents

Preface

The title of this volume „Women, Communication, and Careers,“ draws attention to interconnections which have received scant scholarly attention. A number of reasons explain this neglect, chief of which are the fact that women's studies have barely entered their second decade and have just recently acquired a sufficiently broad research base to suggest that women may approach work and careers differently from men. The question why this is so led social psychologists to amass information on sex-based differences in childhood training, school experiences, educational preparation and life goals. All of these differences in turn pointed to differentially structured social values and expectations governing women's and men's lives which are reinforced by the media.

At the 27th Congress of the International Communications Association (ICA) in Berlin in 1977, the two editors decided to explore the interconnections between women, communication, and careers in a more systematic manner. The topic had recently been suggested by the International Association of Women in Radio and Television. In Munich, media personnel had wondered whether and how the electronic media view women's careers. Questions had also been raised whether media emphasis on traditional roles inhibited career choices. Some of these and other issues, focussing on the growing number of women pursuing careers in business corporations, were treated in the Berlin session, other papers were solicited later.

The volume is unique in three respects; it is based on shared sex-related concerns among a group of researchers in widely differing fields; it is interdisciplinary; and it utilizes and incorporates research traditions from both sides of the Atlantic. Though the nine contributors received traditional and discipline-based university educations, they all noted that sex was a crucial though previously largely unresearched factor in much psychological and social explanation. How it affects media programming, career patterns and expectations, and what role it plays in everyday communications strategies needs further illumination.

The volume is interdisciplinary in that it brings together studies from a variety of fields. *Hoffman, Dorr, Lesser,* and *Sturm* have degrees in social psychology. *Wartella* and *Robinson* are trained mass communications scholars, while *Jelinek* and *Frost* are management experts, and *Grewe-Partsch* is a lawyer. In addition to that, the studies reflect common research traditions and outlooks evolved in both North America and Europe. They interpret empirical findings in a historico-philosophical context, lending depth and perspective to career studies which have frequently been viewed as isolated job steps rather than as ongoing life patterns.

The contributions of this volume may be divided into three main categories. The first two articles deal with the way in which female children are prepared for their working lives. The next three focus on media definitions of women's work and behavior. The final two articles cover female/male management experiences and differences in career communications patterns. *Hoffman's* socialization article notes that differences in attitudes toward work originate in childhood where girls learn early that relatives, friends, and teachers have lower achievement expectations of them than of their brothers. In their review of literature *Dorr* and *Lesser* in turn document that even very young children are aware of, and generally accept, the world of work, the prestige hierarchy for occupations, and the stereotypes for who can hold which occupations.

In the articles dealing with the media, *Wartella* notes that television mothers are unidimensional, pro-social characters, and stereotyped as the soothing caretakers of their families. They generally tend to be overshadowed in importance by their husbands and/or children. *Sturm* and *Grewe-Partsch* suggest that television inhibits the emergence of an active and emancipated attitude toward women's work by a stereotypical selection, treatment and presentation mode. Entertainment and advertising content overwhelmingly represents women in the home, while political reporting "symbolically" annihilates them by either ignoring their public contributions or by mentioning them as dependents. The short term, mosaic presentation mode furthermore suggests that women's activities are properly portrayed as short term. Such a perspective in turn cultivates a piecemeal approach to work which undermines the development of proper career goals and preparation.

Robinson's analysis of thirty years' of magazine portrayal of women and work suggests that print has been more responsive to the growing labor force participation of women than the electronic media. The women's movement has legitimated work and non-traditional jobs, though the division of labor in the patriarchal family remains largely unexplored. The large number of articles dealing with discriminations in access and promotion and the attention devoted to difficulties at the work place justify cautious optimism that public attitudes toward women and work are changing.

The final two articles raise questions about measures women can take to overcome their lack of knowledge of the rules of the corporate game. Proper assessment of capabilities, the use of mentors, and career planning are presented as essential components for success. On the interpersonal level women must also become aware of how their communication styles differ from those of men, when conflict situations need resolving.

Knowing how to parry attacks while standing one's ground and ultimately presenting one's own point of view effectively is clearly a talent women must learn in order to achieve their goals. Such knowledge also contributes to building a social world in which all humans will have a better chance of understanding and appreciating each other.

Gertrude Joch Robinson

Lois Wladis Hoffmann

Early childhood experiences and women's achievement motives*

The failure of women to fulfill their intellectual potential has been adequately documented. The explanations for this are so plentiful that one is almost tempted to ask why women achieve at all. Their social status is more contingent on whom they marry than what they achieve; their sense of femininity and others' perception of them as feminine is jeopardized by too much academic and professional success; their husband's masculinity, and hence their love relationship as well as their reciprocal sense of femininity, is threatened if they surpass him; discrimination against women in graduate school admittance and the professions puts a limit on what rewards their performance will receive; their roles as wives and mothers take time from their professional efforts and offer alternative sources of self-esteem. Perhaps most important, they have an alternative to professional success and can opt out when the going gets rough. A full scale achievement effort involves painful periods of effort and many a man would drop out if that alternative were as readily available as it is to women. But women's underachievement must have roots deeper even than these, for the precursors of the underachieving woman can be seen in the female child.

Even at preschool age girls have different orientations toward intellectual tasks than do boys. Little girls want to please; they work for love and approval; if bright, they underestimate their competence. Little boys show more task involvement, more confidence, and are more likely to show IQ increments. Girls have more anxiety than boys and the anxiety they have is more dysfunctional to their performance. There are also differences in the specific skills of each sex: Males excel in spatial perceptions, arithmetical reasoning, general information, and show less set-dependency; girls excel in quick-perception of details, verbal fluency, rote memory, and clerical skills.

Boys and girls enter the world with different constitutional make-ups, and recent studies show that parents treat boys and girls differently even from birth. Social roles are first – and most impressively – communicated through parent-

---

* This article was first published in: Journal of Social Issues, 28/1972/2.

child relations and events in early childhood may have an impact that cannot later be duplicated in effectiveness.

As a result, interest in women's intellectual achievement has led a number of people to look to the child development data for insights. A few of the limitations of these data will be discussed first, for a number of extravagant generalizations are being drawn from them.

Limitations of child development data

Relativity

Child development data are often relative to a given group. Thus a statement about girls who are „high on aggression" usually means high relative to the other girls studied. If they are compared to boys who are „high on aggression" even in the same study, the actual aggressive behavior may be very different. Boys are considerably more aggressive than girls; a girl who is high on aggression may resemble a boy whose aggressive behavior is coded as average. She may also differ from the boys with respect to the form of aggression and the personality syndrome of which it is a part. It should not be surprising then to discover that the antecedent conditions of high aggression are different in boys and girls. They might very well be different even if the dependent variables were identical, but the fact is that they are not. We are comparing oranges with apples and discovering to our surprise that they grow on different trees.

This problem not only applies to the dependent variables, but also to the independent variables studied, usually parent behavior or the parent-child relationship. To use an actual finding, *Kagan* and *Moss* (1962) found that maternal protectiveness during the first three years was negatively related to adult achievement behavior for girls. This was not true for boys and in fact the relationship was positive although not statistically significant. This is an important finding to which we will return, but here it should be pointed out that we cannot tell from these correlations whether or not the actual maternal behavior is different for high achieving boys and girls. Girls are subject to more overprotection than boys and the same amount of protective behavior may be relatively low for a girl but average or high for a boy.

Baumrind (1970) has pointed out that obtaining data on the differential treatment (or behavior) of boys and girls is difficult because, even in behavioral observations, when the observer knows the sex of the child, „an automatic adjustment is made which tends to standardize judgments about the two sexes."

Generalizability

The problem of generalizing results obtained with one population to another occurs throughout the social sciences. It is particularly acute when the variables involve relative terms. "High parental coerciveness" in a middle class sample may not be considered high in a lower class sample. Furthermore, most empirical generalizations hold only within certain contexts. Variations in social class, parent education, rural-urban residence, family structure, and ethnicity – as well as changes over time – may make the generalizations inapplicable.

As an interesting case in point, it is impossible to generalize white sex differences to blacks for the patterns of sex differences are very different in the two groups. Studies of blacks will be important in interpreting the etiology of sex differences in intellectual performance for in many ways the black male resembles the white female. For both, school performance has been largely irrelevant to adult goals and there are interesting similarities in the patterns of achievement scores that may reflect this (*Tulkin*, 1968; *Jensen*, 1970). In a study of conformity and perceptual judgment by *Iscoe, Williams,* and *Harvey* (1964), black males and white females were more influenced by others than were black females and white males. Similarities between black males and white females argue against constitutional explanations, for these two groups share neither hormones nor race – but they do share environmental handicaps.

Maturation

Another difficulty in interpreting sex differences among children pertains to differences in the maturity of boys and girls. The newborn girl is one month to six weeks developmentally ahead of the boy. At school entrance she is about one year ahead, depending on the index of growth used. Growth does not proceed equally on all fronts and the intellectual growth rate is not related to the physical (*Bayley*, 1956). These different degrees of maturity complicate the comparison between the sexes.

Conceptualization

Ambiguous concepts are a problem in many fields. The so-called inconsistencies in the child development data often upon close examination turn out to be inconsistencies in the researcher's summaries and concluding statements rather than in the actual findings. If examined in terms of the operational definitions, contradictory studies sometimes turn out to be dealing with different phenomena that have been given the same label. Among the particularly troublesome concepts that are important in the sex-difference literature are identification and dependency (*Bronfenbrenner*, 1960; *Maccoby* and *Masters*, 1970).

Female achievement orientations

There are very few studies that have empirically connected socialization experiences to sex differences in achievement orientations. As a matter of fact, there are few studies of sex differences in child rearing practices in general, and existing data – most of which were originally collected for other purposes – are subject to the limitations mentioned above. Promising new approaches sensitive to identifying sex differences may be found in the studies of parent-child interaction with neonates (*Moss*, 1967; *Moss* and *Robson*, 1968; *Moss, Robson*, and *Pedersen*, 1969; *Lewis*, 1969; *Goldberg* and *Lewis*, 1969; *Kagan*, 1969; *Kagan, Levine*, and *Fishman*, 1967). These are mainly longitudinal studies which will make their most valuable contributions in the future, but some have already examined relationships between maternal behavior and cognitive orientations.

Probably the richest current area in the study of sex differences has to do with cognitive styles. *Witkin, Dyk, Faterson, Goodenough*, and *Karp* (1962) as well as other investigators have been interested in differences in perceptions of and approaches to problems. For example, some people are more affected by background stimuli than others. In a task in which the subject is asked to line up a rod until it is perpendicular, the fact that the frame around the rod is tilted will affect the judgment of some respondents more than others. Those most affected by the tilting frame are said to be field dependent. This body of research has revealed a number of personality traits that are associated with performance on the task, and a number of cognitive skills such as mathematical ability that seem to be closely tied to field independence. These personality traits describe differences between the sexes; the corresponding cognitive abilities similarly differentiate.

For example, *Maccoby* (1963, 1966)[1] has pointed out that girls are more conforming, suggestible, and dependent upon the opinions of others. These traits in turn have been related to field dependency, inability to break the set of a task, and IQ's that tend to decrease rather than increase over the years. She suggests that these same traits in females might also account for their superior performance on spelling and vocabulary tests, and their inferior performance on tests involving analytic thinking, spatial ability, and arithmetic reasoning. Additional discussion on this issue can be found in *Kagan* (1964), *Sherman* (1967), *Silverman* (1970), and *Kagan* and *Kogan* (1970).

The actual linkage between these personality traits and the cognitive styles has not been established, nor has the etiology of sex differences in personality. Some of the infancy studies mentioned above are making inroads. Thus the finding that mothers spend more time in face-to-face verbalizations with infant girls (*Kagan,* 1969; *Moss,* 1967; *Goldberg* and *Lewis,* 1969) may be tied to the observation that female infants are more verbally responsive and to the later superiority of females in verbal ability. Verbal responsiveness may also result from the fact that girls' hearing is superior to that of boys (*Garai* and *Scheinfeld,* 1968). Also relevant is a study with 10-year-olds in which observations of mother-daughter interaction in task solving showed that girls good in math or spatial relations were left to solve tasks by themselves while the mothers of girls higher on verbal skills (the more typical female pattern) were more intrusive with help, suggestions, and criticism (*Bing,* 1963).

The present paper will focus on an area that is even less explored: the question of motivation for top intellectual performance. There are data that the very brightest women more often than comparable men stop short of operating at their top intellectual level. *Terman* and *Oden* (1947) have shown that gifted girls did not as adults fulfill their potential as often as gifted boys. *Rossi* (1965a, 1965b) has summarized data indicating that even those few women who do go into science and the professions rarely achieve eminence[2].

These data reflect in part the factors mentioned earlier – alternative choices in life that have been available to women but not to men, barriers to career opportunities that exist because of women's family roles, and discrimination in the professions which limits the rewards obtainable. The concern here is not with these factors, however, but with a deeper, more psychologically-based motivation that occurs in women. The most relevant data come from the work of *Horner* (1968, 1972) who has demonstrated with a projective story completion measure a „fear of success" among able college women. Furthermore, women who indicate fear of success show poorer performance in a competitive task than when the same task is performed alone. In interpreting her results, *Horner* suggests that this fear exists in women because their anticipation of success is accompanied by the anticipation of negative consequences in the form of social rejection or loss of femininity.

The idea that the affiliative motive can be dysfunctional to performance is supported by another of *Horner's* findings. Men who were motivated both to achieve and to affiliate showed a performance decrement when asked to compete with another man. *Horner* suggests this decrement may have resulted from a conflict of motives since "out-performing a competitor may be antagonistic to making him a friend."

Affiliative needs and achievement

There is a great deal of evidence that females have greater affiliative needs than males (*Oetzel*, 1966; *Walberg*, 1969) and therefore the conflict between affiliation and achievement probably will occur more often for women. It seems that, apart from direct concerns with whether or not their behavior is sufficiently "feminine", academic and professional women frequently allow their concern with affective relationships to interfere with the full use of their cognitive capacities. In group discussion and in intellectual argument, women often seem to sacrifice brilliance for rapport.

However, while the findings of the *Horner* studies (1972) and our observations of professional women focus attention on the dysfunctions of affiliative motivations for performance, there are data indicating that the desire for love and approval can also have a positive effect. In fact, the *Crandalls* (V. J. *Crandall*, 1963; V. C. *Crandall*, 1964) as well as others (*Garai* and *Scheinfeld*, 1968) have suggested that achievement behavior in girls is motivated not by mastery strivings as with boys, but by affiliative motives.

In two very different studeis, nursery school and elementary school girls' achievement efforts were motivated by a desire for social approval to a greater extent than were boys'. In the nursery school study the attempt was also made to motivate the children by appeals to mastery strivings; this technique succeeded with boys but failed with girls (*Lahtinen*, 1964). In the study with elementary school children, achievement motives in boys were related positively to achievement test scores. Among the girls, affiliative motives, not achievement motives, were so related (*Sears*, 1962, 1963). Other studies with nursery school and elementary school children found affiliative behavior and achievement efforts positively related in girls, but boys showed no such relationship (*Tyler, Rafferty,* and *Tyler,* 1962; *Crandall, Dewey, Katkovsky,* and *Preston,* 1964). Similarly with adult women, the achievement arousal techniques that are effective with males have failed with females (*Veroff, Wilcox,* and *Atkinson,* 1953; *Horner,* 1968), but appeals to social acceptability have been successful (*Field,* 1951). ·

There are also several studies that indicate that throughout grade school boys are more motivated than girls to master challenging tasks when social approval is not involved. When given the opportunity to perform an easy or more difficult task, to work on a puzzle they had already solved or one they had failed, to pursue further or escape a difficult problem, boys are more likely to choose the more difficult and challenging, girls to choose the task that promises easy success or to leave the scene (*Crandall* and *Rabson*, 1960; *Moriarty*, 1961; *McManis*, 1965; *Veroff*, 1969).

From these studies it appears that female achievement behavior even at pre-school or early grade school ages is motivated by a desire for love rather than mastery. When achievement goals conflict with affiliative goals, as was the case in *Horner's* projective responses and in the competitive situation in which her fear-of-success girls showed less competent performance, achievement behavior will be diminished and/or anxiety result. This does not mean that academic performance is lower for females in general since it is often compatible with affiliative motives. In elementary schools, excellence is rewarded with love and approval by parents, teachers, and peers. Even in the lower socioeconomic class, sociometric studies show that academic excellence in girls is rewarded with popularity (*Glidewell* et al., 1966; *Pope*, 1953). In college, however, and in professional pursuits, love is less frequently the reward for top performance. Driving a point home, winning an argument, beating others in competition, and attending to the task at hand without being side-tracked by concern with rapport require the subordination of affiliative needs.

In short, the qualities needed for sustained top performance – especially as an adult – are not typically part of a girl's make-up. She wants approval and so she performs well in school. She works for good grades. And indeed throughout grammar school, high school, and college, she obtains higher grades than boys (*Oetzel*, 1966; *Garai* and *Scheinfeld*, 1968). If overachievement is thought of as grades exceeding IQ's, then girls as a group are more overachieving than boys. But girls are less likely to become involved in their task; they are less motivated by strivings for mastery. In *McClelland's* sense of achievement (*McClelland, Atkinson, Clark,* and *Lowell*, 1953) – competition with a standard of excellence – they fall short[3].

This affiliative need may be particularly germane to achievement patterns because it may be rooted in early experiences when the child is learning patterns of effectance. When little boys are expanding their mastery strivings, learning instrumental independence, developing skills in coping with their environment and confidence in this ability, little girls are learning that effectiveness – and even safety – lie in their affectional relationships. The idea expressed by *Kagan*

(1964) that boys try to "figure the task" and girls try to "figure the teacher" seems rooted in early childrearing practices and reinforced by later experiences.

Statement of theory

It is the thesis here that the female child is given inadequate parental encouragement in early independence strivings. Furthermore, the separation of the self from the mother is more delayed or incomplete for the girl because she is the same sex with the same sex role expectations, and because girls have fewer conflicts with their parents. As a result, she does not develop confidence in her ability to cope independently with the environment. She retains her infantile fears of abandonment; safety and effectiveness lie in her affective ties. These points will now be elaborated and supportive data brought in where available.

The development of independence, competence, and self-confidence

All infants are dependent; as the child matures his independence strivings increase. Observers have often been impressed with what *White* (1960) calls the *effectance motive* – the child's need to have an effect upon his environment. Thus the child grasps and releases, reaches and pulls, and in the course of doing this he learns about his environment and his ability to manipulate it. He develops cognitive abilities, and he develops a sense of effectiveness – a sense of competence through increasingly successful interaction with his environment.

As the infant matures, the feats he undertakes get scarier. Increasingly they involve separating the self from the mother and leaving the security of that unity. Early independence explorations seem to take place most successfully with the parent present; the child moves toward independence so long as the "safety man" is in sight. As he gains confidence, the parent's presence becomes less and less necessary.

Very likely this period – somewhere between a year and three or four years of age – is critical in the development of independence and competence (*Erikson,* 1959; *Veroff,* 1969; *White,* 1960; *Stendler,* 1963). By critical, we mean a period when independence and competence orientations are more efficiently learned than at other times. There is a rapid building up of notions about the self and about the world.

Although theories differ as to the exact timing and differential importance of the events occurring in this period, all would probably agree on the minimal requirements for the development of independence and competence. Thus if the infant is deprived of affection, rejected, or prematurely pushed toward independence, he will not have a secure base from which to build true independence. The dependency that results from a short shrift in early affective ties is probably of a distinct kind (*Stendler, 1963*). We do not think it is more characteristic of girls, nor that it is sufficiently common to the nonpathogenic middle class family to be useful in understanding prevalent female achievement orientations.

Even with an adequate affective base, independent behavior does not happen automatically. It requires not only opportunities for independent behavior but also actual parental encouragement. Evidence for this can be found in *Baumrind's* research (*Baumrind* and *Black*, 1967; *Baumrind*, 1971) which indicates that competence comes not from permissiveness but from guidance and encouragement. The first steps a child takes are exciting but also frightening, and cues from the mother can greatly influence the subsequent behavior. The mother's delight is part of her independence training; her apprehension constitutes training in dependence.

Further, if the child's early independence behaviors are to be followed by more, these ventures must be reasonably in accord with his abilities. Repeated successes such as these will have the important effect of developing in the child a sense of competence. There may be a delicate timing mechanism – premature independence can backfire; but the parent who withholds independence opportunities too long and indeed does not encourage independent behavior will also fail to produce an independent child. (It is possible that the appropriate timing is different for boys than girls due to differences in abilities and maturation rates.)

The awareness that the mother is a separate person whose wishes are not the same as his serves to increase the child's striving for autonomy and independence. Both *Erikson* and *White* see the period between one and three as the battle for autonomy. At this age the child's motoric explorations often require parental interference. The span of consecutive action is such that interference can be frustrating for the child and completions gratifying. Toilet training usually occurs around this time. The child thus enters into conflict with his mother; out of this conflict, if it does not involve his humiliation and defeat, the child will emerge with "a lasting sense of autonomy and pride" (*Erikson, 1959*) and "a measure of confidence in his own strength" (*White, 1960*).

The empirical findings

Independence training: Sex differences

Early exploratory behaviors in which the child interacts effectively with his environment are seen here as crucial in building up a sense of competence. In this respect males have a number of advantages.

Infant studies. Studies of neonates suggest a higher activity level on the part of the male, while females demonstrate greater tactile sensitivity and a lower pain threshold (*Garai* and *Scheinfeld,* 1968). From these predispositions alone we could expect more exploratory behavior on the part of male infants, but to compound the matter observations of mothers with neonates show that even controlling for the differences in activity levels, mothers handle and stimulate males more than females (*Moss,* 1967, undated). A study by *Rubenstein* (1967) suggests that such maternal attentiveness facilitates exploratory behavior.

Kagan and *Lewis* and their associates have also reported differences in maternal behavior toward male and female infants (*Kagan, Levine,* and *Fishman,* 1967; *Goldberg* and *Lewis,* 1969). Whether the maternal behavior is primarily a response to infant predispositions or a cause of the differences is not definitely established, but there is some evidence that both influences occur. That maternal behavior is not entirely a response to the infant is indicated by relationships found between the mother's infant care and her orientations prior to the child's birth. For example, *Moss* (1967) reports that mothers were interviewed two years before they gave birth and rated on their attitudes toward babies. A positive attitude toward babies was found to relate significantly to the amount of responsiveness later shown to her 3-week-old infant. This same investigator also found mutual visual regard – one of the earliest forms of mother-infant communication – to be related to maternal attitudes expressed before the birth (*Moos* and *Robson,* 1968). On the other hand, that maternal behavior is not the sole determinant of the infant's behavior is indicated by the fact that the sex differences in tactile stimulation and pain thresholds mentioned above have been established for infants less than four days old and still in the hospital nursery (*Garai* and *Scheinfeld,* 1968; *Silverman,* 1970). An interaction hypothesis seems most tenable in the light of the present data.

One of *Moss's* mother-infant interaction findings is particularly pertinent to the theory presented in this paper (1967; undated). He reports data on the mother's responsiveness to the infant's cries and notes that this sequence – baby cries and mother responds with the needed care – is important in shaping the infant's response to the mother as a supplier of comfort. The more closely the mother's caretaking behavior is related to the infant's cries, the more effectively will the child "regard the mother as having reinforcing properties and respond to her accordingly (*Moss*, undated, p. 10)." The correlation obtained between maternal contact and infant irritability was statistically significant for females but not for males. The mothers did not attend to the female infants more than the male (less, in fact) but their attention was more closely linked to the infant's state of need as expressed by crying. This finding if borne out by further research could be very important for several reasons. First, it could signify the beginning of a pattern of interaction between mothers and daughters in which the daughters quickly learn that the mother is a source of comfort; and the mother's behavior is reinforced by the cessation of crying. The sheer presence of the mother would soon signal the satisfaction of the infant's needs. Second, there is agreement among most investigators that there are critical periods in infancy when learning takes place so efficiently that long range behaviors are effected by simple but pertinently timed events; this might be such a critical period. Third, even if this is not a critical period, the finding may reflect an orientation of mothers toward daughters that is often repeated beyond the infancy period.

In any case, one thing appears certain from this body of research on early mother-infant interaction: There are sex differences in both maternal and infant behavior during the first year of life. That sex role learning is begun so early should not be surprising. Sex is a primary status – the first one announced at birth. The mother is very much aware of it. Her early behaviors toward the infant are not deliberate efforts to teach the child his proper sex role, but she has internalized society's view and acts accordingly. She acts toward her son as though he were sturdy and active and she is more likely to show pleasure when his behavior fits this image. Her daughter is her doll – sweet and delicate and pink. The mother's behavior reflects this perception, and if the child exhibits behavior consistent with the female stereotype, such as dependency, she is not as likely to discourage it as she would with a son.

Independence training in childhood. Moving from early infancy, we find studies that link independence training and the parent's achievement orientations to the child's competence (*Baumrind* and *Black,* 1967) and achievement orientations (*Winterbottom,* 1968; *Rosen* and *D'Andrade,* 1959), but few examining sex differences in the independence and achievement training children receive. It is our view that because of parental attitudes toward male and female children which reflect their culturally assigned roles, males receive more effective independence training and encouragement.

An adaptation of the *Winterbottom* measure for use with parents of younger children was developed by *Torgoff* (1958). Using this measure, *Collard* (1964) asked mothers of 4-year-olds to indicate the ages they thought parents should expect or permit certain child behaviors. For example, the parents were asked at what age they believed parents should: (a) begin to allow their child to use sharp scissors with *no* adult supervision, (b) begin to allow their child to play away from home for long periods of time during the day without first telling his parents where he will be. The answers to these questions yielded two measures – *independence granting* and *achievement induction*. Mothers of girls responded with later ages than mothers of boys. This difference was significant for the independence-granting items and it was particularly strong in the middle class. The achievement induction scores were not significantly different for the two sexes, but close inspection of the data revealed that, for the middle class, mothers of girls indicated an earlier age for only two of the 18 items making up the scale. One of the two exceptions was "sharing toys" which may have more to do with inter-personal relationships than with achievement.

Parental anxiety and protectiveness. Still another difference in the independence training received by boys and girls may stem from parental ambivalence: Parents may show more unambivalent pleasure in sons' achievements than in daughters'. The young child's first motoric adventures can produce anxiety in the mother as well as the child, just as they produce pleasure for both. It seems likely that for the parent of a boy there is a particular pride in the achievement and less of a feeling of the child's fragility; as a result there is a clearer communication of pleasure in the achievement per se. A beaming mother when the child takes his first steps may have a very different effect than the mother who looks anxious while holding out loving arms. In the former case, the task itself becomes the source of pleasure (in reinforcement terms the reward is closer to the act). In the latter case, the mother is saying in effect, "You may break your neck en route, but I will give your love when you get here." The mother's indications of anxiety as the child moves toward independence make the child doubt his own competence, for mothers are still omniscient to the young child.

There is some indirect evidence for this view. Despite the greater maturity and sturdiness of the female infant (*Garai* and *Scheinfeld,* 1968), parents think of them as more fragile. Furthermore, behavioral observations of infants have shown that male infants are handled more vigorously (*Moss,* 1967). The setting of later ages for granting autonomy to girls, as indicated in the *Collard* (1964) study mentioned earlier, suggests that parents are more protective, if not more anxious, toward girls. For example, parents report allowing boys to cross busy streets by themselves earlier, though they are not motorically more advanced than girls and their greater motoric impulsivity would seem to make this more dangerous. And we do know that infants pick up the subtle attitudes of their caretakes. This was demonstrated in the well-known study by *Escalona* (1945) in which the infant's preference for orange or tomato juice depended heavily on the preference of the nurse who regularly fed him. The infant had no way of knowing his nurse's preference except through sensing her attitude as she fed him.

Another kind of parent behavior that is detrimental to the development of independence might be called *over-help*. Mastery requires the ability to tolerate frustration. If the parent responds too quickly with aid, the child will not develop such tolerance. This shortcoming – the tendency to withdraw from a difficult task rather than to tackle the problem and tolerate the temporary frustration – seems to characterize females more than males. This has been demonstrated in the test situations mentioned earlier, and *Crandall* and *Rabson* (1960) have also found that, in free play, grade school girls are more likely than boys to withdraw from threatening situations and more frequently to seek help from adults and peers. The dysfunctions of this response for the development of skills and a sense of competence are clear. There are no data to indicate that over-help behavior is more characteristic of parents of girls, but such a difference seems likely in view of the greater emphasis placed on the independence training of boys.

Clearly more research is needed to identify differences in the independence and achievement training – and in any overprotection and over-help – that parents provide boys and girls. Even if the differences we have described are definitely established, it will still need to be shown that this pattern of parental protectiveness and insufficient independence training is a major contributor to an inadequate sense of personal competence in girls. It should be pointed out, however, that this inference is consistent with the findings that girls are more anxious than boys, more likely to underestimate their abilities, and more apt to lack confidence in their own judgment when it is contrary to that of others (*Sarason*, 1963; *Sarason* and *Harmatz*, 1965; *Sears*, 1964; *Crandall*, *Katkovsky*, and *Preston*, 1962; *Hamm* and *Hoving*, 1969). There is also evidence that the above pattern is reinforced by the later socialization experiences of girls. Several investigators report that while dependency in boys is discouraged by parents, teachers, peers, and the mass media, it is more acceptable in girls (*Kagan* and *Moss*, 1962; *Kagan*, 1964; *Sears, Rau,* and *Alpert*, 1965). Data from the Fels study (*Kagan* and *Moss*, 1962) are particularly interesting in this respect, reporting that childhood dependency predicted to adult dependency for females but not males, the converse being true for aggression. Their interpretation is that pressure is exerted on the child to inhibit behaviors that are not congruent with sex role standards (*Kagan*, 1964).

Establishing a separate self: Sex differences

Same sex parent as primary caretaker. Separation of the self is facilitated when the child is the opposite sex of the primary caretaker. *Parsons* (1949, 1965) and *Lynn* (1962, 1969), as well as others, have pointed out that both males and females form their first attachment to the mother. The girl's modeling of the mother and maintaining an identity with her is consistent with her own sex role, but the boy must be trained to identify with his father or to learn some abstract concept of the male role. As a result, the boy's separation from the mother is encouraged; it begins earlier and is more complete. The girl, on the other hand, is encouraged to maintain her identification with the mother; therefore she is not as likely to establish an early and independent sense of self. If the early experiences of coping with the environment independently are crucial in the development of competence and self-confidence, as suggested previously, the delayed and possibly incomplete emergence of the self should mitigate against this development.

There are no studies that directly test this hypothesis. As indirect evidence, however, there are several studies showing that the more indentified with her mother and the more feminine the girl is, the less likely she is to be a high achiever and to excel in mathematics, analytic skills, creativity, and game strategies. For example, *Plank* and *Plank* (1954) found that outstanding women mathematicians were more attached to and identified with their fathers than their mothers. *Bieri* (1960) found that females high on analytical ability also tended to identify with their fathers. Higher masculinity scores for girls are related positively to various achievement measures (*Oetzel*, 1961; *Milton*, 1957; *Kagan* and *Kogan*, 1970), as are specific masculine traits such as aggressiveness (*Sutton-Smith, Crandall,* and *Roberts*, 1964; *Kagan* and *Moss*, 1962). The relation between cross-sex identification and cognitive style for both boys and girls is discussed also by *Maccoby* (1966).

For several reasons the above studies provide only limited support for our view. First, there is some evidence, though less consistent, that "overly masculine" males, like "overly feminine" females, are lower on various achievement-related measures (*Maccoby,* 1966; *Kagan* and *Kogan,* 1970). Second, the definitions and measures of femininity may have a built-in anti-achievement bias. Third, the question of the mother's actual characteristics has been ignored; thus the significant factor may not be closeness to the mother and insufficient sense of self, as here proposed. The significant factor may be identifying with a mother who is herself passive and dependent. If the mother were a mathematician, would the daughter's close indentification be dysfunctional to top achievement?

Clearly the available data are inadequate and further research is needed to assess the importance of having the same sex as the primary caretaker for personality and cognitive development.

Parent-child conflict. Establishing the self as separate from the mother is also easier for boys because they have more conflict with the mother than do girls. Studies of neonates suggest, as mentioned above, that males are more motorically active; this has also been observed with older children (*Garai* and *Scheinfeld,* 1968; *Moss,* 1967; *Goldberg* and *Lewis,* 1969). Furthermore, sex differences in aggressive behavior are solidly established (*Oetzel,* 1966; *Kagan,* 1964), and there is some evidence that this is constitutionally based (*Bardwick,* 1971). Because of these differences, the boy's behavior is more likely to bring him into conflict with parental authority. Boys are disciplined more often than girls, and this discipline is more likely to be of a power assertive kind (*Becker,* 1964; *Sears, Maccoby,* and *Levin,* 1957; *Heinstein,* 1965). These encounters facilitate a separation of the self from the parent. (While extremely severe discipline might have a very different effect, this is not common in the middle class.)

One implication of this is that girls need a little maternal rejection if they are to become independently competent and self-confident. And indeed a generalization that occurs in most recent reviews is that high achieving females had hostile mothers while high achieving males had warm ones (*Bardwick,* 1971; *Garai* and *Scheinfeld,* 1968; *Maccoby,* 1966; *Silverman,* 1970). This generalization is based primarily on the findings of the Fels longitudinal study (*Kagan* and *Moss,* 1962). In this study "maternal hostility" toward the child during his first three years was related positively to the adult achievement behavior of girls and negatively to the adult achievement behavior of boys. Maternal protection, on the other hand, as mentioned earlier, related negatively to girls' achievement and positively to boys'.

In discussions of these findings „maternal hostility" is often equated with rejection. There is reason to believe, however, that it may simply be the absence of „smother love." First, the sample of cooperating families in the Fels study is not likely to include extremely rejecting parents. These were primarily middle class parents who cooperated with a child development study for 25 years. They were enrolled in the study when the mother was pregnant, and over the years they tolerated frequent home visits each lasting from 3 to 4 hours, as well as behavioral observations of their children in nursery school and camp. Second, we have already pointed out that what is "high hostility" toward girls, might not be so labeled if the same behavior were expressed toward boys. It is interesting to note in this connection that "high hostility" toward girls during these early years is related positively to "acceleration" (i.e., the tendency to push the child's cognitive and motoric development) and negatively to maternal protectiveness. Neither of these relationships is significant for the boys (*Kagan* and *Moss*, 1962, p. 207). Further, the mothers who were "hostile" to their daughters were better educated than the "nonhostile." In addition to being achievers, the daughters were "less likely to withdaw from stressful situations" as adults. The authors themselves suggest that the latter "may reflect the mother's early pressure for independence and autonomy [p. 213]."

Our interpretation of these findings then is that many girls experience too much maternal rapport and protection during their early years. Because of this they find themselves as adults unwilling (or unable) to face stress and with inadequate motivation for autonomous achievement. It is significant that the relationships described are strongest when the early years are compared to the adult behavior. Possibly the eagerness to please adults sometimes passes as achievement or maturity during the childhood years.

While excessive rapport between mother and son occurs, it is less common and usually of a different nature. The achievement of boys may be in greater danger from too much conflict with parents – there being little likelihood of too little.

The danger for girls of too much maternal nurturance has been pointed out by *Bronfenbrenner* (1961a, 1961b) and is consistent with data reported by *Crandall, Dewey, Katkovsky,* and *Preston* (1964). The finding that girls who are more impulsive than average have more analytic thinking styles while the reverse pattern holds for boys also fits this interpretation (*Sigel,* 1965; *Kagan, Rosman, Day, Phillips,* and *Phillips,* 1964). That is, impulsive girls may be brought into more conflict with their mothers, as in the typical pattern for boys. *Maccoby* (1966) has suggested that the actual relationship between impulsivity and analytic thinking is curvilinear: The extreme impulsivity that characterizes the very impulsive boys is dysfunctional, but the high impulsivity of the girls falls within the optimal range. In our view, the optimal range is enough to insure some conflict in the mother-child relationship but not so much as to interfere with the child's effective performance.

Inadequate self-confidence and dependence on others

Since the little girl has (a) less encouragement for independence, (b) more parental protectiveness, (c) less cognitive and social pressure for establishing an identity separate from the mother, and (d) less mother-child conflict which highlights this separation, she engages in less independent exploration of her environment. As a result she does not develop skills in coping with her environment nor confidence in her ability to do so. She continues to be dependent upon adults for solving her problems and because of this she needs her affective ties with adults. Her mother is not an unvarying supply of love but is sometimes angry, disapproving, or unavailable. If the child's own resources are insufficient, being on her own is frustrating and frightening. Fears of abandonment are very common in infants and young children even when the danger is remote. Involvement in mastery explorations and the increasing competence and confidence that results can help alleviate these fears, but for girls they may continue even into adulthood. The anticipation of being alone and unloved then may have a particularly desperate quality in women. The hypothesis we propose is that the all-pervasive affiliative need in women results from this syndrome.

Thus boys learn effectance through mastery, but girls are effective through eliciting the help and protection of others. The situations that evoke anxiety in each sex should be different and their motives should be different.

The theoretical view presented in this paper is speculative but it appears to be consistent with the data. In the preceding sections we have reviewed the research on sex differences in early socialization experiences. The theory would also lead us to expect that owing to these differences females would show less self-confidence and more instrumental dependency than males.

The data on dependency are somewhat unclear largely because the concept has been defined differently in different studies. These findings have been summarized by *Kagan* (1964), *Oetzel* (1966), *Garai* and *Scheinfeld* (1968), and the concept of dependency has been discussed by *Maccoby* and *Masters* (1970). The balance of the evidence is that females are more dependent, at least as we are using the concept here, and this difference appears early and continues into maturity. *Goldberg* and *Lewis* (1969) report sex differences in dependency among one-year-olds, but *Crandall* and his associates (*Crandall, Preston,* and *Rabson,* 1960; *Crandall* and *Rabson,* 1960) found such differences only among elementary school children and not among preschoolers. It should be noted, however, that even differences that do not show up until later can have their roots in early experiences. For example, independence training at a later age may require a sense of competence based on early successes if it is to be effective.

The findings on self-confidence show that girls, and particularly the bright ones, underestimate their own ability. When asked to anticipate their performance on new tasks or on repetition tasks, they give lower estimates than boys and lower estimates than their performance indicates (*Brandt,* 1958; *Sears,* 1964; *Crandall, Katkovsky,* and *Preston,* 1962; *Crandall,* 1968). The studies that show the girls' greater suggestibility and tendency to switch perceptual judgments when faced with discrepant opinions are also consistent with their having less self-confidence (*Iscoe, Williams,* and *Harvey,* 1963; *Allen* and *Crutchfield,* 1963; *Nakamura,* 1958; *Hamm* and *Hoving,* 1969; *Stein* and *Smithells,* 1969)[4]. Boys set higher standards for themselves (*Walter* and *Marzolf,* 1951). As mentioned earlier, difficult tasks are seen as challenging to males, whereas females seek to avoid them (*Veroff,* 1969; *Crandall* and *Rabson,* 1960; *Moriarty,* 1961; *McManis,* 1965). Thus the research suggests that girls lack confidence in their own abilities and seek effectance through others (*Crandall* and *Rabson,* 1960). Affective relationships under these conditions would indeed be paramount.

The findings indicating that this is the case – that affective relationships are paramount in females – were summarized earlier in this paper. The data suggest that they have higher affiliative needs and that achievement behavior is motivated by a desire to please. If their achievement behavior comes into conflict with affiliation, achievement is likely to be sacrificed or anxiety may result.

Implications

If further research provides support for the present developmental speculations, many questions will still need answering before childrearing patterns used with girls can be totally condemned. Even from the standpoint of achievement behavior, I would caution that this paper has only dealt with the upper end of the achievement curve. Indices of female performance, like the female IQ scores, cluster closer to the mean and do not show the extremes in either direction that the male indices show. The same qualities that may interfere with top performance at the highest achievement levels seem to have the effect of making the girls conscientious students in the lower grades. Is it possible for the educational system to use the positive motivations of girls to help them more fully develop their intellectual capacities rather than to train them in obedient learning? The educational system that rewards conformity and discourages divergent thinking might be examined for its role in the pattern we have described.

Although childrearing patterns that fail to produce a competent and self-confident child are obviously undesirable, it may be that boys are often prematurely pushed into independence. Because this paper has focused on achievement orientations, it may seem that I have set up the male pattern as ideal. This is not at all intended. The ability to suppress other aspects of the situation in striving for mastery is not necessarily a prerequisite for mental health or a healthy society. The more diffuse achievement needs of women may make for greater flexibility in responding to the various possibilities that life offers at different stages in the life cycle. A richer life may be available to women because they do not single-mindedly pursue academic or professional goals. And from a social standpoint, a preoccupation with achievement goals can blot out consideration of the effect of one's work on the welfare of others and its meaning in the larger social scheme.

A loss in intellectual excellence due to excessive affiliative needs, then, might seem a small price to pay if the alternative is a single-minded striving for mastery. But the present hypothesis suggests that women's affiliative needs are, at least in part, based on an insufficient sense of competence and as such they may have a compelling neurotic quality. While I have not made the very high achievement needs more characteristic of males the focus of this paper, they too may have an unhealthy base. By unraveling the childhood events that lead to these divergent orientations we may gain insights that will help both sexes develop their capacities for love and achievement.

Footnotes

[1] These reviews by *Maccoby* and reviews by *Kagan* (1964), *Becker* (1964), *Glidewell, Kantor, Smith,* and *Stringer* (1966), *Oetzel* (1966), *Garai* and *Scheinfeld* (1968), *Silverman* (1970), *Kagan* and *Kogan* (1970), and *Bardwick* (1971) will be referred to throughout the paper where a point is supported by several studies that are adequately reported in the review.

² *Simon, Clark,* and *Galway* (1970), on the other hand, have reported that the woman PhD who is employed full time publishes as much as her male colleagues.

³ Women have obtained scores on *McClelland's* test of achievement motivation under neutral conditions that are as high or higher than those obtained by men under arousal conditions; however, researchers have questioned the validity of the measure for women (see *McClelland* et al., 1953; and *Horner,* 1968).

⁴ Girls do not conform more to peer standards which conflict with adult norms (*Douvan* and *Adelson,* 1966), even though they conform more when group pressure is in opposition to their own perceptual judgments.

References

Allen, V.L.; Crutchfield, R.S.: Generalization of experimentally reinforced conformity. In: Journal of Abnormal and Social Psychology, 67/1963/–, pp. 362 – 333.

Bardwick, Judith M.: Psychology of women. A study of bio-cultural conflicts. New York: Harper and Row 1971. VII, 242 p.

Baumrind, D.: Socialization and instrumental competence in young children. In: Young Children, –/1970/Dec., pp. 9 – 12.

Baumrind, D.; Black, A.E.: Socialization practices associated with dimensions of competence in preschool boys and girls. In: Child Development, 38/1967/–, pp. 291 – 327.

Baumrind, Diana: Current patterns of parental authority. Washington, D.C.: American Psychological Association 1971. 103 p.

Bayley, N.: Growth curves of height and weight by age for boys and girls, scaled according to physical maturity. In: Journal of Pediatrics, 48/1956/–, pp. 187 – 194.

Bayley, N.: Developmental problems of the mentally retarded child. In: Philips, Irving (ed.) et al.: Prevention and treatment of mental retardation. New York: Basic Books 1966.

Becker, W.: Consequences of different kinds of parental discipline. In: Hoffmann, M.L. (ed.) et al.: Review of child development research, vol. 1. New York: Russell Sage 1964.

Bieri, J.: Parental identification, acceptance of authority and within-sex differences in cognitive behavior. In: Journal of Abnormal and Social Psychology, 60/1960/–, pp. 76 – 79.

Bing, E.: Effect of childrearing practices on development of differential cognitive abilities. In: Child Development, 34/1963/–, pp. 631 – 648.

Brandt, R. M.: The accuracy of self-estimate. A measure of self concept. In: Genetic Psychology Monographs, 58/1958/–, pp. 55 – 99.

Bronfenbrenner, Urie: Freudian theories of identification and their derivatives. in: Child Development, 31/1960/–, pp. 15 – 40.

Bronfenbrenner, Urie: Some familial antecedents of responsibility and leadership in adolescents. In: Petrullo, Luigi (ed.) et al.: Leadership and interpersonal behavior. New York: Holt, Rinehart and Winston 1961. (a)

Bronfenbrenner, Urie: Toward a theoretical model for the analysis of parent-child relationships in a social context. In: Glidewell, John C. (ed.): Parental attitudes and child behavior. Springfield, Ill.: Thomas 1961. (b)

Coleman, James Samuel: The adolescent society. The social life of teenagers and its impact on education. New York: Free Press of Glencoe 1961. XVI, 368 p.

Collard, E.D.: Achievement motive in the four-year-old child and its relationship to achievement expectancies of the mother. Ann Arbor, Mich., Univ. of Michigan, diss. 1964.

Crandall, V.C.: Achievement behavior in young children. In: Young Children, 20/1964/–, pp. 77 – 90.

Crandall, V.C.: Sex differences in expectancy of intellectual and academic reinforcement. In: Smith, Charles P. (ed.): Achievement-related motives in children. New York: Russell Sage Foundation 1969.

Crandall, V.J.: Achievement. In: Stevenson, Harold W. (ed.): Child psychology. The 62nd yearbook of the National Society for the Study of Education, part 1. Chicago: Univ. of Chicago Press 1963.

Crandall, V.J. (coll.); *Dewey, R.* (coll.); *Katkovsky, W.* (coll.) et al.: Parents' attitudes and behaviors and grade school children's academic achievements. In: Journal of Genetic Psychology, 104/1964/–, S. 53 – 66.

Crandall, V.J.; Katkovsky, W.; Preston, A.: Motivational and ability determinants of young children's intellectual achievement behaviors. In: Child Development, 33/1962/–, S. 643 – 661.

Crandall, V.J.; Preston, A.; Rabson, A.: Maternal reactions and the development of independence and achievement behavior in young children. In: Child Development, 31/1960/–, pp. 243 – 251.

Crandall, V.J.; Rabson, A.: Children's repetition choices in an intellectual achievement situation following success and failure. In: Journal of Genetic Psychology, 97/1960/–, pp. 161 – 168.

Douvan, Elizabeth M.; Adelson, Joseph: The adolescent experience. New York: Wiley 1966. XII, 471 p.

Erikson, Erik Homburger: Identity and the life cycle. New York: International Universities Press 1959. 171 p.

Escalona, S.K.: Feeding disturbances in very young children. In: American Journal of Orthopsychiatry, 15/1945/–, pp. 76 – 80.

Field, William Franklin: The effects on thematic apperception of certain experimentally aroused needs. College Park, Md., Univ. of Maryland 1951. IX, 184 p.

Garai, J.E.; Scheinfeld, A.: Sex differences in mental and behavioral traits. In: Genetic Psychology Monographs, 77/1968/–, S. 169 – 299.

Glidewell, J.C. (coll.); *Kantor, M.B.* (coll.); *Smith, L.M.* (coll.) et al.: Socialization and social structure in the classroom. In: Hoffmann, L.W. (ed.) et al.: Review of child development research, vol. 2. New York: Russell Sage 1966.

Goldberg, S.; Lewis, M.: Play behavior in the year old infant. Early sex differences. In: Child Development, 40/1969/–, p. 21 – 31.

Hamm, N.K.; Hoving, K.L.: Conformity of children in an ambiguous perceptual situation. In: Child Development, 40/1969/–, pp. 773 – 784.

Heinstein, Martin I.: Child rearing in California. A study of mothers with young children. Berkeley, Calif.: Bureau of Maternal and Child Health, State of Calif., Dept. of Health 1965. 98 p.

Horner, M.S.: Toward an understanding of achievement related conflicts in women. In: Journal of Social Issues, 28/1972/2.

Horner, Matina Souretis: Sex differences in achievement motivation and performance in competitive and non-competitive situations. Ann Arbor, Mich., Univ. of Michigan, diss. 1968. Ca. 246 p.

Iscoe, I.; Williams, M.; Harvey, J.: Modifications of children's judgements by a simulated group technique. A normative developmental study. In: Child Development, 34/1963/–, pp. 963 – 978.

Iscoe, I.; Williams, M.; Harvey, J.: Age, intelligence and sex as variables in the conformity behavior of Negro and White children. In: Child Development, 35/1964/–, pp. 451 – 460.

Jensen, A.R.: The race x sex x ability interaction. Berkeley, Calif.: Univ. of Calif. 1970.

Kagan, J.: Acquisition and significance of sex-typing and sex-role identity. In: Hoffmann, M.L. (ed.) et al.: Review of child development research, vol. 1. New York: Russell Sage 1964.

Kagan, J.: On the meaning of behavior. Illustrations from the infant. In: Child Development, 40/1969/–, pp. 1121 – 1134.

Kagan, J.; Kogan, N.: Individuality and cognitive performance. In: Mussen, Paul H. (ed.): Carmichael's manual of child psychology, vol. 1. New York: Wiley 1970.

Kagan, J.; Levine, J.; Fishman, C.: Sex of child and social class as determinants of maternal behavior. Paper presented at the Meeting of the Society for Research in Child Development, March 1967. N.P.: n. pr. 1967.

Kagan, Jerome; Moss, Howard A.: Birth to maturity. A study in psychological development. New York: Wiley 1962. 381 p.

Kagan, Jerome (coll.); *Rosman, B.L.* (coll.); *Day, D.* (coll.) et al.: Information processing in the child. Significance of analytic and reflective attitudes. Washington, D.C.: American Psychological Association 1964. 37 p.

Lahtinen, Pirkko Maija-Leena: The effect of rejection and failure on children's dependency. Ann Arbor, Mich., Univ. of Michigan, diss. 1964. Ca. 101 p.

Lewis, M.: Infants' responses to facial stimuli during the first year of life. In: Developmental Psychology, 1/1969/–, pp. 75 – 86.

Lynn, D.B.: Sex role and parental identification. In: Child Development, 33/1962/–, pp. 555 – 564.

Lynn, David Brandon: Parental and sex role identification. Berkeley, Calif.: McCutchan 1969. VII, 131 p.

Maccoby, Eleanor E.: Woman's intellect. In: Farber, Seymour M. (ed.) et al.: Man and civilization. The potential of women. A symposium. New York: McGraw-Hill 1963.

Maccoby, Eleanor E.: Sex differences in intellectual functioning. In: Maccoby, Eleanor E. (ed.): The development of sex differences. Stanford, Calif.: Stanford Univ. Press 1966.

Maccoby, Eleanor E.; Masters, J.C.: Attachment and dependency. In: Mussen, Paul H. (ed.): Carmichael's manual of child psychology, vol. 2. New York: Wiley 1970.

McClelland, David C. (coll.); *Atkinson, J.W.* (coll.); *Clark, R.A.* (coll.) et al.: The achievement motive. New York: Appleton-Century-Crofts. 1953. XXII, 384 p.

McManis, D.L.: Pursuit-rotor performance of normal and retarded children in four verbal-incentive conditions. In: Child Development, 36/1965/–, pp. 667 – 683.

Milton, G.A.: The effects of sex-role identification upon problem solving skill. In: Journal of Abnormal and Social Psychology, 55/1957/–, pp. 208 – 212.

Moriarty, A.: Coping patterns of preschool children in response to intelligence test demands. In: Genetic Psychology Monographs, 64/1961/–, pp. 3 – 127.

Moss, H.A.: Laboratory and field studies of mother-infant interaction. Rockville, Md.: National Institute of Mental Health n.d.

Moss, H.A.: Sex, age, and state as determinants of mother-infant interaction. In: Merrill-Palmer Quarterly, 13/1967–, pp. 19 – 36.

Moss, H.A.; Robson, K.S.: Maternal influences in early social visual behavior. In: Child Development, 39/1968/–, pp. 401 – 408.

Moss, H.A.; Robson, K.S.; Pedersen, F.: Determinants of maternal stimulation of infants and consequences of treatment for later reactions to strangers. In: Developmental Psychology, 1/1969/–, pp. 239 – 247.

Nakamura, C.Y.: Conformity and problem solving. In: Journal of Abnormal and Social Psychology, 56/1958/–, pp. 315 – 320.

Oetzel, R.M.: The relationship between sex role acceptance and cognitive abilities. Stanford, Calif., Stanford Univ., masters thesis 1961.

Oetzel, R.M.: Annotated bibliography and classified summary of research in sex differences. In: Maccoby, Eleanor E. (ed.): The development of sex differences. Stanford, Calif.: Stanford Univ. Press 1966.

Parsons, Talcott: Essays in sociological theory pure and applied. Glencoe, Ill.: Free Press 1949. XIII, 366 p.

Parsons, Talcott: Family stucture and the socialization of the child. In: Parsons, Talcott (ed.) et al.: Family socialization and interaction process. Glencoe, Ill.: Free Press 1960.

Plank, E.H.; Plank, R.: Emotional components in arithmetic learning as seen through autobiographies. In Eissler, R.S. (ed.) et al.: The psychoanalytic study of the child, vol. 9. New York: International Universities Press 1954.

Pope, B.: Socio-economic contrasts in children's peer culture prestige values. In: Genetic Psychology Monographs, 48/1953/–, pp. 157 – 220.

Rosen, B.C.; D'Andrade, R.: The psychosocial origins of achievement motivations. In: Sociometry, 22/1959/–, pp. 185 – 218.

Rossi, A.S.: Barriers to the career choice of engineering, medicine, or science among American women. In: Mattfeld, Jacquelyn A. (ed.) et al.: Women and the scientific professions. Papers presented at the M.I.T. Symposium on American Women in Science and Engineering, 1964. Cambridge, Mass.: Mass. Institute of Technology Press 1965. (a)

Rossi, A.S.: Women in science. Why so few? In: Science, 148/1965/–, pp. 1196 – 1202. (b)

Rubenstein, J.: Maternal attentiveness and subsequent exploratory behavior in the infant. In: Child Development, 38/1967/–, pp. 1089 – 1100.

Sarason, I.G.: Test anxiety and intellectual performance. In: Journal of Abnormal and Social Psychology, 66/1963/–, pp. 73 – 75.

Sarason, I.G.; Harmatz, M.G.: Test anxiety and experimental conditions. In: Journal of Personality and Social Psychology, 1/1965/–, pp. 499 – 505.

Sears, P.S.: Correlates of need achievement and need affiliation and classroom management, self concept, and creativity. Stanford, Calif.: Stanford Univ. 1962.

Sears, P.S.: Self-concept in the service of educational goals. In: California Journal of Instructional Improvement, 7/1964/–, pp. 3 – 17.

Sears, Pauline Snedden: The effect of classroom conditions on the strength of achievement motive and work output of elementary school children. Final report, cooperative research project. U.S. Dept. of Health, Education and Welfare, Office of Education, Washington, D.C. Stanford, Calif.: Stanford Univ. 1963. XVIII, 311, 79 p.

Sears, Robert Richardson; Maccoby, Eleanor E.; Levin, Harry: Patterns of child rearing. Evanston, Ill.: Row, Peterson 1957. 549 p.

Sears, Robert Richardson; Rau, Lucy; Alpert, R.: Identification and child rearing. Stanford, Calif.: Stanford Univ. Press 1965. XIII, 383 p.

Sherman, J.A.: Problems of sex differences in space perception and aspects of intellectual functioning. In: Psychological Review, 74/1967/–, pp. 290 – 299.

Sigel, I.E.: Rationale for separate analyses of male and female samples on cognitive tasks. In: Psychological Record, 15/1965/–, pp. 369 – 376.

Silverman, J.: Attentional styles and the study of sex differences. In: Mostofsky, David L. (ed.): Attention. Contemporary theory and analysis. New York: Appleton-Century-Crofts 1970.

Simon, R.J.; Clark, S.M.; Galway, K.: The woman Ph. D. A recent profile. Paper prepared for a workshop of the New York Academy of Sciences, New York, Feb. 1970. N.P.: n. pr. 1970.

Stein, A. H.; Smithells, J.: Age and sex differences in children's sex role standards about achievement. In: Developmental Psychology, 1/1969/–, pp. 252 – 259.

Stendler, C.B.: Critical periods in socialization. In: Kuhlen, Raymond G. (ed.) et al.: Psychological studies of human development, 2d ed. New York: Appleton-Century-Crofts 1963.

Sutton-Smith, B.; Crandall, V.J.: Roberts, J.M.: Achievement and strategic competence. Paper presented at the Meeting of the Eastern Psychological Association, April 1964. N.p.: n.pr. 1964.

Terman, Lewis Madison; Oden, Melita H.: The gifted child grows up. Twenty-five years' follow-up of a superior group. Stanford, Calif.: Stanford Univ. Press 1947. XIV, 448 p.

Torgoff, I.: Parental development timetable. Paper presented at the Meeting of the American Psychological Association, Washington, D.C., August 1958. N.p.: n. pr. 1958.

Tulkin, S. R.: Race, class, family, and school achievement. In: Journal of Personality and Social Psychology, 9/1968/–, pp. 31 – 37.

Tyler, F.B.; Rafferty, J.E.; Tyler, B.B.: Relationships among motivations of parents and their children. In: Journal of Genetic Psychology, 101/1962/–, pp. 69 –81.

Veroff, J.: Social comparison and the development of achievement motivation. In: Smith, Crandall P. (ed.): Achievement-related motives in children. New York: Russell Sage 1969.

Veroff, J.; Wilcox, S.; Atkinson, J.W.: The achievement motive in high school and college age women. In: Journal of Abnormal and Social Psychology, 48/1953/–, pp. 108 – 119.

Walberg, H.J.: Physics, femininity, and creativity. In: Developmental Psychology, 1/1969/–, pp. 47 – 54.

Walter, L.M.; Marzolf, S.S.: The relation of sex, age, and school achievement to levels of aspiration. In: Journal of Educational Psychology, 42/1951/–, pp. 258 – 292.

White, R.W.: Competence and the psychosexual stages of development. In: Jones, M. (ed.) Nebraska Symposium on Motivation. Lincoln, Neb.: Univ. of Nebraska Press 1960.

Winterbottom, M.R.: The relation of need for achievement to learning experiences in independency and mastery. In: Atkinson, John William (ed.): Motives in fantasy, action and society. A method of assessment and study. Princeton, N.J.: Van Nostrand 1958.

Witkin, Herman A. (coll.); *Dyk, R.B.* (coll.); *Faterson, H.F.* (coll.) et al.: Psychological differentiation. Studies of development. New York: Wiley 1962.

Aimee Dorr, Gerald S. Lesser

Career awareness in young children*

Introduction

Most research on career development and most efforts to provide career education begin in adolescence when an individual approaches the point of a career decision. In this chapter we contend that our attentions ought also to be given to much younger children. We support this recommendation by reviewing literature which shows that even very young children are aware of, and generally accept, the world of work, the prestige hierarchy for occupations, and the stereotypes for who can hold which occupations. In this review we limit ourselves to the United States and ask that the reader always supply this qualification to our statements even though we will avoid repetitive inclusion of it. While we are thus somewhat ethnocentric in our focus, we are nonetheless talking about the lives of millions of people who are strongly influenced by the occupational structure within which they find themselves.

Since nearly all the males and half of the females in American society work for thirty to forty years, occupation determines what may matter most to an individual – how one spends the greatest portion of one's time on earth. One's occupation consumes many hours per week for about half one's life. In addition it affects standard of living, hours of leisure, set of friends, where one lives and what kind of family life one has. It channels one's ultimate contribution to society and one's satisfaction or dissatisfaction with that contribution.

Occupation defines status, both in one's own eyes and in the eyes of others – with the prestige attached to different occupations showing a remarkable similarity in almost all the countries of the world. Even after the thirty- or forty-year period of employment, one's occupation remains one's defining characteristic: "retirement" is defined as the absence of occupation.

---

* This chapter is based on an earlier report: Leifer, Aimee Dorr; Lesser, Gerald S.: The development of career awareness in young children. Prepared under a grant from the Education and Work Program, National Institute of Education. Cambridge, Mass.: Harvard Graduate School of Education 1976. Unpublished manuscript[1].

It is beyond dispute that women and minorities fill a disproportionately large number of lower-status occupations, earning lower salaries and receiving less recognition for their contributions to society (e.g., *Waldman* and *McEaddy,* 1974). For example, the average full-time salary for all male workers was $7,664 in 1968, while the full-time salary for all working women was $4,457 (U.S. Department of Labor, 1970). Although absolute amounts of income have risen since that time for both men and women (accompanied, of course, by even larger increases in the cost of living), women remain at the same relative disadvantage.

This relative disadvantage is shared, of course, by members of minority groups, where minority groups are defined as peoples of color rather than as white ethnics. The causes of the occupational disadvantages experienced by minorities probably differ from those for women, but some of the outcomes are similar. For example, the average yearly salaries for minority men and women are lower than those for white men: minority men average about 65 % of a white male's salary and minority women about 45 % of a white male's salary (*Kreps,* 1971). The median combined income of a working husband and a working wife in a black family is less than the median income of white families whether or not the wife works (*Gump* and *Rivers,* 1973; *Hill,* 1971; *Monthly Labor Review,* 1975).

These salary differentials between men and women and between whites and minorities are due both to the fact that the various groups are disproportionately distributed among occupations and to the fact that the various groups often receive different salaries when they are similarly employed. This latter inequity of unequal pay for equal work is relatively easy to redress through the enactment and enforcement of appropriate laws. The former inequity of occupations being closed to women and minorities, is much more difficult to redress because it requires changes in all segments of the society in aspirations, education, and stereotypes. Such changes may be facilitated by career education programs; however, the necessary changes probably differ for each sex and ethnic group.

Because the range of personal and social determinants of one's occupation is so great and varies for each individual, we have little general understanding of why inequities persist. The individual, often without clear reasons, moves toward certain careers and away from others, ordinarily failing to consider many other options because of their unfamiliarity or invisibility. At the same time, several social, political, and economic gatekeepers operate to facilitate or block the person's movements in these different directions. Where one happens to grow up, the careers that were possible or prominent there, the occupations of parents and neighbors, the formal and informal training opportunities in the community, the job opportunities available in the community, all these forces seem to conspire to put the career decision beyond a person's conscious control. The operation of these many factors is indeed complex. Existing theories of vocational choice do, however, provide some leads in understanding the complexities.

Theoretical approaches to occupational choice

Three major theoretical approaches to occupational choice are evident in the literature, with each highlighting one aspect of career involvement: (1) social, political, and economic forces, (2) occupational demands, and (3) personal characteristics. What is finally needed, and not yet available, is a theoretical structure which incorporates all three approaches into one coherent whole.

Social, political, and economic forces

Powerful social, political, and economic forces affect occupational choice. Operating in America today, they are all implicated in some way in employment patterns and the manner in which particular individuals fit into those patterns. Although sociologists, political scientists, government officials, and economists have been attempting for decades to decipher the operation of these forces, they are especially difficult to comprehend, shifting continuously and affecting individuals differently at different points in their careers.

A partial list of social influences – which themselves may reflect political and economic conditions – conveys their complexities: parental, peer, and school influences; occupational models available in the community, including parents, relatives, and neighbors; general standard of living in the surrounding community; rate and direction of social mobility; ease or difficulty of migration; availability of training and apprenticeship opportunities; desirability of local residential areas. Such influences were discussed as early as the 1950's by sociologists such as *Miller* and *Form* (1951), who summarized them in their discussion of the effects of (or accidents of) birth, and *Caplow* (1954), who capsulated them into the effects of parents and education. Today *Jencks* et al. (1972) continue this tradition.

It seems likely, however, that the foremost social reason for the unequal occupational status of women and minorities is obvious and persistent job discrimination, i.e., the unwillingness of employers to accept female and minority employees on equal terms with white males. It seems likely that the bases for such discrimination may differ somewhat for females and minorities, but we have little understanding of the fundamental causes of discrimination. Some recent political changes can be noted; pressures against job discrimination have mounted, "affirmative action" programs have been implemented. It remains to be seen, however, how much effect these recent actions will have.

Political forces at the federal, state, and local levels all affect employment patterns and occupational choice. The partial or complete government regulation of certain industries, the absence of regulation of others, political patronage in job appointments, government control of certain job-training opportunities and not others – all are examples of political influences. Economic forces are just as massive and complex: the general state of the economy at both national and local levels, the shifting demands for certain goods and services, the cycles of inflation and recession, the personal finances of individuals that make access to only certain occupations feasible.

Occupational demands

Another approach to understanding the complexities of occupations is that of industrial psychologists, engineers, and vocational analysts who attempt detailed observations and descriptions of what activities are demanded by different occupations, how the efficiency of these activities can be improved and their cost reduced. As helpful to industry as these descriptions and recommendations may be, they rarely help to make career choice more informed on a widespread scale. Seldom are career choices made by matching the demands of various occupations with the personal skills and interests of those selecting them, although the rationality of such a decision-making process is apparent.

There have in the past been descriptions of occupational activities which have guided vocational education programs and testing, as well as one or two current attempts to provide such a structure. The *Dictionary of Occupational Titles* (1949, U.S. Employment Service, Division of Occupational Analysis) and its revision (*Fine* and *Heinz,* 1957, 1958) served such a function. Today, the fifteen occupational clusters devised by the Office of Education have helped structure some career education curricula. Some theorists, most notably *Holland* (1966), have analyzed the characteristics of occupations and personal hierarchies of habitual or preferred ways of dealing with the necessary tasks of living, in order to test the idea that individuals choose occupations whose activities match their more habitual or preferred styles (see *Osipow, Ashby,* and *Wall,* 1966, and *Stockin,* 1964, for sample tests of this theory). Such approaches may be helpful in structuring career education curricula and counseling and deserve fuller attention than they have as yet received.

Personal characteristics

Educators, psychologists, and vocational-guidance experts also have studied career choice, focusing primarily upon the personal characteristics that seem to operate. The effect of certain personal characteristics upon career choice is well-established, including the individual's "preferences" and "interests," "abilities" and "aptitudes," "aspirations" and "expectations," "motives" (e.g., *Roe,* 1956) and "values," "self-concept" and "feelings of competence" (e.g., *Ginzberg* et al., 1951; *Super,* 1957; *Tiedeman* and *O'Hara,* 1963).

Despite the many personal attributes that have been considered, other more pragmatic individual characteristics have been largely ignored. How much does the individual know about what careers exist and about their appropriateness and accessibility? How much does the person know about the occupational realities and their fit to personal attributes? Given the very limited first-hand experience that children receive concerning the realities of occupations, their knowledge of what occupations exist and what personal demands they make is apt to be incomplete, distorted, and stereotypic. The application of individual "interests," "motives," "values," and the like to such limited knowledge about occupations can only result in limited or inaccurate career decisions.

Other pragmatic personal characteristics involve the family. What financial resources does a family have to invest in the training and job entry of its members? How willing is the family to make these investments? When family resources are insufficient for the training of all its members, how are decisions made about fair allocation? Such personal considerations have not yet been studied.

Perhaps the most influential personal characteristics in career choice are sex and minority-group status. Available evidence clearly indicates that white girls and boys differ in their occupational aspirations and in personal characteristics that seem most related to occupational attainment. There is considerable less comparative information on the personal characteristics and occupational aspirations of the various minority-group and majority children and of the two sexes within each minority group. What there is is mixed in its conclusions.

40

Thus, while it seems likely that sex and minority-group status are highly influential in occupational choice, our conclusions about minority children must be more tentative than those about girls.

Sex differences in personal characteristics of white children appear very early in their games and "avocations." Girls' games usually involve low risk, taking turns, indirect competition, accommodation, and inclusiveness whereas boys' games emphasize high risk, physical contact, intrusiveness, and competition leading to a clear designation of winners and losers (*Lee* and *Gropper,* 1974; *Sutton-Smith,* 1972). From earliest childhood, boys are expected to develop instrumental competencies, while girls develop interpersonal sensibilities and skills (*Baumrind,* 1972; *Maccoby* and *Jacklin,* 1974).

Even in the absence of specific information about occupations, girls in the early grades seem to know that they are operating at a disadvantage. We have little evidence on children as young as preschoolers, but girls in early elementary-school grades show a far narrower range of aspired to occupations than do boys, with most studies reporting that boys select two to three times as many different occupations as girls and that roughly two-thirds of the girls at this age level choose either teacher or nurse (*Boynton,* 1936; *Clark,* 1967; *Deutsch,* 1960; *Looft,* 1971; *Nelson,* 1968; *Siegel,* 1973). From kindergarten through the sixth grade, girls report that women can work only in certain occupations, such as nurse, waitress, or librarian, while men are not similarly limited (*Schlossberg* and *Goodman,* 1972), and it is much more common for girls than boys to suggest that spouse and parent will be their major adult occupational roles.

The effects of minority-group status are generally less clear and certainly not differentiated for each of the major minority groups within the United States. While occupational attainment is clearly lower for minorities, the aspirations of minority parents for their children (*Baughman* and *Dahlstrom,* 1968; *Cloward* and *Jones,* 1963; *Deutsch,* 1965; *Gurin* and *Katz,* 1966; *Herriott* and *St. John,* 1966; *Reiss* and *Rhodes,* 1959; *Scanzoni,* 1971) and of young minority children for themselves (*Antonovsky,* 1967; *Deutsch,* 1960; *Gray,* 1944; *Kuvlesky* and *Thomas,* 1971; *Nelson,* 1968) are generally as high as those held for and by white children. In fact, when social class and intelligence are held constant, aspirations may be higher for blacks than for whites (*Barnett* and *Baruch,* 1973; *Boyd,* 1952; *Nelson,* 1968). However, there also is some indication that black children and presumably other minority children, particularly prior to the black power movement, may devalue their own group in comparison to whites (*Crooks,* 1971; *Koslin* et al., 1969; *Morland,* 1962, 1972) and that blacks underestimate their own abilities and other personal qualifications to advance educationally and to enter a high status professional occupation (e.g., *Wylie,* 1963). Thus, for minority children, we do not see the same early acceptance of lower occupational attainment that we saw for girls, although there may be a similar devaluation of their own competency. Surely both groups come to an early recognition of the stereotyped and discriminatory patterns of occupational attainment among adults today, and this must at some point affect their own aspirations and expectations.

The intersection of causes

As important as the expansion of early career awareness may prove to be, it is the intersection of this awareness with many personal, social, and economic forces that ultimately must be understood. This combination of influences upon career choice is illustrated in several studies (e.g., *Wright* et al., 1972) that compare the low occupational status of Mexican-Americans with that of other groups. Personal characteristics are implicated: language difficulties, subcultural values (e.g., non-competitiveness) that are highly respected in their subculture but hinder achievement in the American mainstream, lack of knowledge of appropriate opportunities for training and job access. Social and political forces operate against Mexican-Americans: fewer supporting formal organizations in the community, fragmented political activism within the local community, and most important, job discrimination in employment. Economically, a low standard of living perpetuates itself from generation to generation, with job discrimination creating the poverty of an earlier generation which virtually guarantees poverty for the next.

Such complex forces operate, in one form or another, in the career decisions of all people. However, researchers from each discipline study only some separate and partial aspect, failing to combine their partial understandings into a sufficiently complete and realistic understanding to guide remedial action. The absence of a broad perspective has prevented our understanding the realities of career choice, especially for women and minorities. For the most part, small groups of middle-class male adults of average or above-average intelligence have been studied, with women and minorities neglected. For women, this has meant that several salient aspects of employment have been largely ignored: age of entry into an occupation, time span of participation (such as number and spacing of interruptions), degree of participation (such as various schedules of part-time involvement), and fulfillment of the demanding roles of worker, spouse and parent. For women and minorities this has meant little attention to the ways in which one deals with high aspiration and achievement in a larger environment which often expects little from one and may block whatever appears.

Research on career awareness also is limited in other ways. Understanding career decisions and their consequences almost demands longitudinal analyses, yet such studies rarely are done. Methods for eliciting information usually employ forced-choice techniques with standard coding categories used to classify the data; we do not know how different the results of these studies would be if more open-ended procedures and other coding schemes were used. The scope, refinement, and precision of our research seem, for several reasons, far less than is necessary to an understanding of career choice.

Adolescence versus childhood

Thus, we know little about how career decisions are made, their antecedents, and the various influences upon them. With so much uncertainty, it is easy to see why the vast majority of efforts in career education and most research have focused on adolescents and young adults. These are the most visible decision points with regard to occupation, the times when one chooses an occupation and embarks upon it or upon the training necessary for it. It is also assumed that occupations are only visible enough to adolescents and young adults, but not to younger children, to allow them to gather meaningful information about careers and to begin to make informed choices.

Such research and career education programs usually fail to consider the precursors to career choice, even though these may strongly influence an adolescent's occupational choice. Many adolescents and young adults may reach this point with insufficient or misleading information and with stereotyped attitudes about occupations and those who hold them. Our failure to take account of the early antecedents to career choice may be especially damaging to women and minorities. In addition to the other obstacles to occupational equality for women and minorities, it is possible that they do not at adolescence choose certain occupations because they do not know about them, do not realize that the occupation may be accessible to them, or do not understand the steps that must be taken to prepare, enter, and succeed in an occupation. Thus, it seems important to consider career awareness among very young children and to trace its development into adolescence and adulthood, and this conviction is strengthened by two lines of evidence from research with young children.

The first line of evidence we use is an argument by analogy. It is the fact that many important attitudes are formed early and persist relatively unchanged throughout life. For example, sex-role attitudes determine many of the choices one makes through life and the content of these stereotypes is acquired by about the age of seven (*Bardwick,* 1971; *Kohlberg,* 1966; *McCandless,* 1969; *Mischel,* 1970; *Mussen,* 1969). Attitudes toward members of other cultural groups are also discernible at or before this age (e.g., *Goodman,* 1964; *Porter,* 1971), as are the precursors of important political attitudes (e.g., *Hess* and *Torney,* 1967; *Hyman,* 1959) and moral judgments (e.g., *Kohlberg,* 1969). This early acquisition of important and lasting attitudes suggests that an awareness of careers and orientations toward them may also be formed quite early in development.

The second reason to consider occupational awareness in young children is the recent direct evidence (cited later) that children as young as five do have attitudes about careers and occupations as well as opinions about the appropriateness of certain careers for them. The fact that many of these attitudes are based on insufficient information, misinformation, or stereotyped perceptions of women and minorities increases the belief that early childhood is an important period for the development of career awareness.

Concepts of career awareness

Even for children as young as three to five years of age, "career awareness" may be composed of several different, but interacting, clusters of information and attitudes. In what follows we will describe these clusters. Although each is illustrated by a series of questions, we do not imply that people ask such questions directly. Rather, these questions and answers are often vague and diffuse, but still affect career choice.

Information

Cluster 1: Information about occupational behavior:
   What occupations exist in our society?
   What do people do in these occupations?
   What skills are required by each occupation?
   Who performs what kinds of work?

Cluster 2: Information about antecedents and social consequences:
   How do people come to occupy these positions?
   What interests and values lead to particular occupations?
   What training is needed?

How is access managed?
What are the lifestyles of people in various occupations?
What is achieved as a consequence of various forms of work?
What are their limitations?

Cluster 3: Information about the self:
What are my capabilities and potentialities?
What are my interests?
What are my values?
What are my tangible and intangible resources for training?

Attitudes

Cluster 4: Attitudes about others and their work:
What values are placed on various types of occupations?
What are the capabilities and potentialities of others?
What are the ,,appropriate" roles for various types of people?

Cluster 5: Attitudes about the self and work:
What types of occupations do I value?
What are the "appropriate" roles for myself?
What value do I place on work *per se?*
What value do the intrinsic and extrinsic rewards of work have?
What value do I give my own capabilities and potentialities?

Along with the information and attitudes in the five preceding clusters, total career development must also include the development of interpersonal, intellectual, and decision-making skills useful in attaining and performing any occupation. Such skill acquisition, however, will not be considered in this paper, since adequate education and socialization of young children would necessarily provide the fundamentals for all the specific skills which might be developed later when tentative occupational choices are being made.

In suggesting our various clusters or elements of career awareness, we are not proposing that young children will learn them in any particular order. We expect that children as young as preschool age will expand their concepts about what is done in specific occupations if this is made visible to them, or that they will learn generalized social attitudes toward work if this is what we choose to teach them. Several studies document the early development of awareness of many different occupations, of their social consequences, and of their "appropriateness" for different people, and it is to these that we now turn.

Information about careers (Clusters 1, 2, 3)

We have very limited knowledge of the career information of children between the ages of four and twelve in any of our three information clusters. Some work has been done on children's knowledge of the skills required by various occupations, and information on children's knowledge of the existence of different occupations can be extrapolated from studies of children's occupational aspirations. There are also a number of studies of children's understanding of the status hierarchy of occupations in the United States. We have not, however, been able to find any studies (except those of sex-role acquisition) of the development of information in our Cluster 3, information about the self, which may be directly related to occupational orientation. As with all of our information on career awareness, there is limited understanding of ethnic differences in such information and somewhat better understanding of sex differences, particularly among white children.

Knowledge of the skills required by various occupations has been found to increase in a sample of third to eleventh graders whose ethnicity was not described (*Nelson,* 1963). Children's awareness of the existence of different occupations also apparently increases with age. Taking the number of occupations aspired to by boys as a rough measure of children's knowledge of existing occupations, one finds that black and white children between the ages of three and five altogether nominate approximately thirteen different occupations (*Kirchner* and *Vondracek,* 1973)[2], first and second grades of unspecified ethnicity nominate eighteen occupations (*Looft,* 1971), and black and white third through sixth graders nominate sixty occupations (*Clark,* 1967). Even sixty occupations is a small number compared to the titles listed in sources such as the *Dictionary of Occupational Titles.* Children, however, may be aware of more occupations than those listed in the occupational aspiration studies from which our estimates were taken.

As children mature they are also increasingly likely to project themselves into adult roles and to define adult roles by occupations. For example, there is a notable increase (from 4 % to 44 %) from the fourth through twelfth grades in the percentage of white, middle-class boys and girls who included occupational role as one of their responses in a self-definition task (*Montemayor* and *Eisen,* 1977). Higher percentages of children who can project themselves into an occupational role are found when they are asked explicitly to do this rather than being in the free-response situation utilized by *Montemayor* and *Eisen* (1977). When black and white preschoolers were asked what they would like to be when they

46

grew up, 57 % of a sample of three-year-olds, 66 % of four-year-olds, and 84 % of five-year-olds projected themselves into an adult role defined by occupation, adult status, or parenthood (*Kirchner* and *Vondracek,* 1973). There is a corresponding increase in projection of one's self into specific occupational roles. In the *Kirchner* and *Vondracek* study, 24 % of the three-year-olds, 34 % of four-year-olds, and 66 % of five-year-olds mentioned one or more specific occupations when asked what they would like to be when they grew up. *Davis, Hagan* and *Strouf* (1962) reported that 60 % of the black and white twelve-year-olds they questioned made tentative occupational choices. Together these studies show an early equating of adulthood with occupational involvement, a willingness to project one's self into an occupational role, an increase throughout childhood and adolescence in conceiving of occupational role as one of the defining characteristics of one's self, and a far from complete concern with occupation even at the end of high school.

Several studies document the early development of awareness about the social consequences of occupations. *Weinstein* (1958), interviewing elementary school students whose ethnicity is not specified, found that they all mentioned occupations as a criterion for social stratification of adults. They also understood that higher status occupations led to greater material rewards. Boys and girls as young as third grade have a very clear understanding of the prestige assigned to various adult occupations (*DeFleur,* 1963; *Nelson,* 1963; *Simmons,* 1962), and their rankings of the prestige of occupations correlate at an astonishingly high level (roughly .90) with adults' rankings of the same occupations (*Hansen* and *Caulfied,* 1969; *Simmons* and *Rosenberg,* 1971).

A recent study documents the early development of awareness about the types of occupations men and women are likely to hold. In it occupations were categorized as masculine, feminine or neutral on the basis of recent census data. White, middle-class first, third and fifth grade boys and girls were then asked "Who can be –?" for each of a number of occupations. Children's responses on a five point scale ranging from "all men" to "all women" were found to correlate .95 with the ratings from census data (*Garrett, Ein* and *Tremaine,* 1977).

Some information is available on differences between boys and girls and among various ethnic groups in the acquisition of information in Clusters 1 (the existence of various occupations) and 2 (their antecedents and social consequences). The study on information about the skills required by various occupations found no differences between boys and girls of unspecified ethnicity at any grade level (*Nelson,* 1963). The studies on occupational aspirations, which are the basis for our information about children's knowledge of the existence of careers, do not permit any inferences about sex or ethnicity differences, although they do point to clear differences in aspirations which will be reviewed in the next section. No differences have been found among white middle-class children, working-class children, and black children in the prestige they assign to various occupations (*Lefebvre* and *Bohn,* 1971).

There may be some differences between the sexes and between blacks and whites in their willingness to project themselves into adult occupational roles, but the data here are mixed. *Kirchner* and *Vondracek* (1973) found that preschool black and white boys and girls were equally likely to project themselves into adult roles, although boys were slightly more likely to define adult roles by specific occupations (59 % of the boys versus 55 % of the girls), and girls were much more likely to define adult roles by parenthood (30 % of the girls versus 6 % of the boys). *Davis, Hagan,* and *Strouf* (1962), on the other hand, found that twelve-year-old black and white girls were more likely than boys to make occupational choices and *O'Hara* (1962) found that 15 % of a large sample of fourth through sixth grade boys of unspecified ethnicity made fantasy choices about the "sort of person [they] want to become," while such choices were negligible among the girls. In the *Kirchner* and *Vondracek* (1973) study of preschoolers, black children were less likely than white children to project themselves into adult roles in general and considerably less likely to project themselves into specific occupational roles (28 % of the blacks versus 57 % of the whites). In the twelve-year-old sample of *Davis, Hagan,* and *Strouf* (1962), however, there was no difference between black and white children's willingness to make tentative occupational choices. None of these studies simultaneously differentiated children on the basis of both race and sex.

All the data that one might wish on young children's information about careers are not available, but what there is suggests that they have limited information about what people do in different occupations and even more limited information about the antecedents and social consequences of occupations. There is a clear understanding and apparent acceptance of the social hierarchy of occupations and, as the next section demonstrates, clear attitudes about the appropriate occupational roles for themselves and probably for various types of people.

Attitudes about careers (Clusters 4, 5)

We have divided children's attitudes about careers into those focusing on others and those focusing on themselves. The literature does not divide itself so neatly into two clusters, nor does it provide us much information other than that on children's own occupational aspirations. That information is, however, quite telling in the strong evidence it presents for white girls' early constriction of aspirations. It also indicates that young black children do *not* constrict their aspirations, suggesting that the limited occupational attainment of blacks in this culture is caused by factors other than their early personal acceptance of limited occupational roles. In this section we review what is known about young children's occupational aspirations after we review their occupational values and their perceptions of appropriate occupational roles for men and women.

Occupational values

Three studies of elementary school children indicate the importance they place on occupations as a source of income and of pursuit of interests. None of them report the ethnicity of the children studied nor do they report examining differences between boys and girls. *Goodson* (1970) found that most of the third through eighth graders she interviewed gave money as the reason for work, with a very few mentioning personal satisfaction. Similarly, *Hales* and *Fenner* (1972) report that fifth, eighth, and eleventh graders valued job security, money, and self-realization most highly in an inventory of work values. Little change in values was found from the fifth through eleventh grades, leading the authors to conclude that work values are already well-established by the fifth grade. Finally, *Creason* and *Schilson* (1970) report that approximately 35 % of the sixth graders they interviewed justified their occupational preferences by simply stating "I like it." The next most frequent reasons were helping people (12 % of the children), getting lots of money (7 %), and personal interest (6 %).

In a study of a large sample of fourth, fifth, and sixth graders of unspecified ethnicity *O'Hara* (1962) found that boys and girls differed in their reported bases for occupational choices. Fifty percent of the time, girls mentioned personal values as the basis for career choices, while boys mentioned values only 30 % of the time. Boys' interests were their main reason for career choice, while interests accounted for only 30 % of girls' reasons. Neither boys nor girls very often referred to their own capacities as reasons for occupational choice.

Thus, there are indications that children in the later years of elementary school understand that one's interests and values are acceptable bases for occupational choice, but they apparently are not very specific about the relationship between their own interests or values and their occupational choices. Very few of them mention the influence of significant other people, which is one of the primary determinants of careers in adults' retrospective reports of occupational choice. Many children also understand that occupations provide income and make this one of their primary work values. There is the suggestion that boys and girls may use somewhat different bases for justifying occupational choice, and there is no information on ethnic differences in values and interests and their relationship to occupational choices.

"Appropriate" occupational roles for others

Five studies have directly examined young children's perceptions of the occupational roles appropriate for others. The four which explored stereotyping occupational roles on the basis of sex all found evidence for it. The *Garrett, Ein,* and *Tremaine* (1977) study referred to earlier indicated that children stereotyped the extent to which men and women could hold particular occupations, such that their views of the capabilities of the two sexes to be any particular thing were in line with the actual distribution of the two sexes in each occupation. *Beuf* (1974) interviewed a mostly white sample of three- to six-year-old boys and girls, asking them among other things what they would be if they were the opposite sex. 65 % of the boys and 73 % of the girls chose sex-stereotypical occupations, and only one boy and one girl chose nontraditional occupations! The breadth of stereotyping is further evidenced by the fact that all the girls could suggest occupations they might hold if they were boys, while many of the boys could not imagine what jobs they might hold if they were girls. The report of a conversation with one preschooler illustrates the boys' perplexity:

> "[He] put his hands to his head and sighed. 'A girl?' he asked. 'A girl?' again. 'Oh, if I were a girl I'd have to grow up to be nothing' " (*Beuf,* 1974).

Utilizing a very different approach, *Cordua, McGraw,* and *Drabman* (1979) showed videotapes of a nurse and a doctor to white, middle-class, five- and six-year-old boys and girls and then asked them to identify who was doctor and who nurse in photographs of the two characters. When a man was the doctor and a women the nurse, all the children identified them correctly. 91 % identified them correctly when both occupations were filled by women. Problems arose, however, when a male had to be identified as a nurse: 31 % correct when doctor and nurse were both males and 22 % correct when the doctor was a woman. The most frequent error was to identify the male nurse as a doctor, suggesting that children believe that males involved in medicine must be doctors.

50

Instead of asking for childrens' recollections of characters' roles and extrapolating acceptability from that, both *Beuf* (1974) and *Schlossberg* and *Goodman* (1972) presented children with pictures of people in an employment situation and asked them to judge their acceptability directly. *Beuf* (1974) used only one picture, that of a female telephone repairperson, and found that 49 % of the three- to six-year-olds stated that was "not OK." The children were, however, more accepting of egalitarian roles within family situations. *Schlossberg* and *Goodman* (1972) presented kindergartners and sixth graders, whose ethnicity is not reported, with drawings of six typically feminine and six typically masculine occupations, asking if both a man and a woman could hold each job. Answers tended to be stereotyped, although children felt that it was more acceptable for men to hold stereotypically feminine occupations than it was for women to hold stereotypically masculine occupations.

Sex, age and ethnicity differences in children's perceptions of appropriate occupational roles for others have been examined in four studies. Of the three studies which looked at sex differences one found none (*Cordua, McGraw,* and *Drabman,* 1979), one found in a sample of black and white, third through fifth graders that boys were less likely than girls to believe that a woman could be their father's boss (*Kleinke* and *Nicholson,* 1979), and one found results which depended on the sex-role stereotyping for the occupation. Here, boys were more stereotyped than girls for occupations which were stereotypically masculine, each sex stereotyped toward his/her own sex for stereotypically neutral occupations, and the sexes did not differ for stereotypically feminine occupations (*Cordua, McGraw,* and *Drabman,* 1979).

Of the four studies which examined age differences one found no differences between five- and six-year-olds (*Cordua, McGraw,* and *Drabman,* 1979) and another found no difference between kindergartners and sixth graders (*Schlossberg* and *Goodman,* 1972). The other two showed less stereotyping among older children (*Garrett, Ein,* and *Tremaine,* 1977; *Kleinke* and *Nicholson,* 1979). Finally, the only study to examine ethnicity (*Kleinke* and *Nicholson,* 1979) found whites to stereotype by sex more than did blacks, although each race was more willing to agree that a same-race rather than other-race woman could be their father's boss.

Together these studies suggest that boys may be somewhat more likely than girls and younger children somewhat more likely than older children to stereotype occupations for others on the basis of sex. They provide no evidence on stereotyping by ethnicity and only the evidence of one study that black children may stereotype by sex less than do white children. They do, however, lend rather strong support to the proposition that children (especially whites who have been primarily studied) stereotype occupations for others by sex. This proposition is further confirmed for whites by the available studies of children's perceptions of appropriate occupations for themselves, to which we now turn.

"Appropriate" occupational roles for one's self

Compared with the rest of our information on career awareness in young children, there is an abundance of information on young children's occupational aspirations for themselves. Comparison of the aspirations of boys and girls and of whites and various minority groups gives us some indication of the occupational roles children consider appropriate for themselves on the basis of their own sex and/or ethnicity and, by extension, of the occupational roles they consider appropriate for others of the same sex and/or ethnicity. The data, however, are still not complete enough for us to understand which occupational roles minority-group children, other than blacks, perceive to be appropriate for themselves.

The literature on sex stereotyping of occupational choices by young white children is the clearest in its import. For example, *Beuf* (1974) shows that even three- to six-year-old, mostly white, boys and girls have adopted current cultural stereotypes about the occupations that they expect to fill when they grow up. 70 % of the boys and 73 % of the girls chose sex-stereotypical jobs for themselves, while only one boy and one girl chose nontraditional jobs. A number of other studies also report sex-stereotypical occupational choices among white boys and girls or among boys and girls whom we presume to be white because their ethnicity is not specified. *Looft* (1971) found that 76 % of first and second grade girls chose to be either teachers or nurses, *O'Hara* (1962) reported that 67 % of fourth through sixth grade girls chose to be teachers, nurses, secretaries, or mothers, and *Deutsch* (1960) found that a sample of fourth through sixth grade girls mostly chose to be nurses or housewives. *Nelson* (1963) reported that third through eleventh graders justified occupational choices on the basis of sex-appropriateness. Finally, two studies conducted almost forty years apart found almost no overlap between the occupational choices of boys and girls in the second grade (*Siegel,* 1973) and in the first through sixth grades (*Boynton,* 1936).

White boys also consistently nominate many more different occupations than do white girls when asked what they expect to do as adults. Using the same group of studies, we find that in the 1930's boys in the first through the sixth grades chose twenty-three different occupational groups with a frequency of five or more instances per group compared to only thirteen for girls (*Boynton*, 1936). That things have not changed much for white children is indicated by more recent studies in which second grade boys chose twice as many occupations as girls (*Siegel*, 1973), boys in the first and second grades chose eighteen different occupations while girls chose only eight (*Looft*, 1971), and boys in the fourth, fifth, and sixth grades made their choices from a wider range of opportunities than did girls (*O'Hara*, 1962).

Further indication of white girls' early foreclosure of occupational options is found in *Looft's* report that fewer girls than boys could suggest alternative occupations if they could not pursue their first choice (*Looft*, 1971). *Beuf* (1974) also found that many girls said that the job they would hold as a boy was the one they really wanted, but they understood they could not hold it because they were girls.

Judging from the results of two studies conducted twenty years apart, black boys and girls do not stereotype their occupational choices in the same ways as white children. Both *Gray* (1944), working with a large sample of six-to fourteen-year-old black boys and girls, and *Clark* (1965), working with a relatively large sample of third through sixth grade black boys and girls, found that girls' occupational aspirations were higher than boys'. In *Clark's* study, as many as 59 % of the academically achieving boys did not choose occupations at as high a level as girls (*Clark*, 1965). The earlier study (*Gray*, 1944) reports one finding similar to that for white children in that there were twenty-six categories for occupations mentioned at least four times by the black boys and only twelve categories mentioned by black girls, but these results are old and so should be viewed with caution. We could find no studies of sex differences in the occupational aspirations of minority group children other than blacks. Given the differences in the choices of black and white boys and girls, we find no basis for extrapolating any research findings to ethnic groups other than those directly studied.

There are two other studies which report sex differences in occupational aspirations, but they combine information from black and white children in such a way as to obscure the occupational preferences of boys and girls within each race. In the *Kirchner* and *Vondracek* (1973) study reviewed earlier, 19 % of the preschool girls as opposed to only 4 % of the boys stated their occupations as "parents" when they grew up. The specific occupational choices mentioned by the girls also showed a much narrower range and a focus on nurse and teacher (38 % of the girls), while the boys had a broader range (although they too focused on visible occupations such as doctor, police officer, and firefighter). Because there were nearly twice as many whites as blacks in the sample, we may surmise that these patterns are due to white rather than black preferences but we cannot be certain. *Clark* (1967), working with black and white children in the upper elementary school grades, also reports sex differences in occupational aspirations for the two races combined. In a large sample of third through sixth graders boys chose sixty occupations and girls about thirty. The careers of teacher and nurse once again accounted for 67 % of the girls' choices.

Young girls also underestimate their own abilities and personal qualifications for entering higher-status occupations. While both boys and girls make decisions at about the same age about higher status occupations, they make them differently. The more prestigious a boy of this age considers an occupation to be, the more likely he is to prefer it, while a girl's occupational preference is either unrelated to her perception of its prestige or negatively related to it (*Barnett*, 1973; *Barnett* and *Baruch*, 1973). If recent changes provoked by women's movements have occurred, they have not yet appeared in the research on the perceptions of young white children.

Studies of young children from different ethnic groups also document the appearance of early career awareness, as evidenced by their occupational aspirations. Comparing blacks and whites, one study of first graders (*Nelson*, 1968) and seven studies including third through sixth graders (*Antonovsky*, 1967; *Boyd*, 1952; *Clark*, 1967; *Deutsch*, 1960; *Gray*, 1944; *Kuvlesky* and *Thomas*, 1971; *Snelbecker* and *Arffa*, 1966) found no differences between blacks and whites in the educational and occupational aspirations of the children. In fact, when IQ and socioeconomic status are controlled, there is evidence that the aspirations of blacks are higher than those of whites for children from the first through sixth grades (*Barnett* and *Baruch*, 1973; *Boyd*, 1952; *Nelson*, 1968).

We found only two studies which examined the occupational aspirations of minority-group children other than blacks. *Hindelang* (1970) found the occupational aspirations of white fourth through sixth graders from working class families to be higher than those of blacks, which were in turn higher than those of Chicanos. Similarly, *Goldblatt* and *Tyson* (1962) found the occupational aspirations of white fourth through sixth graders of lower socioeconomic status to be higher than those of blacks which were in turn higher than those of Puerto Ricans. Since these two studies are the only ones of ten comparisons of blacks and whites which reported lower occupational aspirations for blacks and the only studies of Chicanos and Puerto Ricans which we found, we do not believe there is a good basis for describing the occupational aspirations of minority-group children other than blacks. The generally high levels of aspirations for blacks do suggest that their pervasive unequal occupational status cannot be attributed to a presumed lower level of aspiration in the early years.

There is also substantial evidence that minority parents are strongly motivated to gain greater educational and occupational opportunities for their children (*Baughman* and *Dahlstrom*, 1968; *Cloward* and *Jones*, 1963; *Deutsch*, 1965; *Gurin* and *Katz*, 1966; *Herriott* and *St. John*, 1966; *Reiss* and *Rhodes*, 1959; *Scanzoni*, 1971). This high level of aspiration, however, is not always accompanied by clear plans for how to help their children to set goals and to take the necessary steps to succeed. Despite the lack of specific plans to achieve their career aspirations, black elementary-school children do realize that they will need to be better educated than whites in order to qualify for the same job (*Hindelang*, 1970).

In addition to their separate effects, sex and race interact in complex ways in affecting early career awareness. Studies conducted more than thirty years ago (e.g., *Boynton*, 1936; *Gray*, 1944) showed black girls, unlike white girls, rarely choosing "housewife" as their future occupation. In recent years, black girls are even more encouraged to aspire to higher level professions and enter the full-time labor force in far greater numbers than white females (*Gump* and *Rivers*, 1973). *Deutsch* (1960) reports that white fourth through sixth grade girls' second most popular occupational choice was housewife, while for black girls it was teacher or whitecollar worker. One-third of the girls of both races chose, however, to be nurses. *Clark* (1967) also found that third through sixth grade black girls expressed higher occupational aspirations than white girls, even when the comparison was between black girls of lower socioeconomic status and white girls of the middle class. As early as the elementary-school level, black girls' occupational aspirations have generally been found to be higher than those of black boys (*Barnett* and *Baruch*, 1973).

All these studies suggest that young children have some awareness of the world of work, but that this understanding, especially for whites, reflects the current, often stereotyped attitudes toward sex and race in that world. We know less about the extent of stereotyping of occupations by ethnicity. Such stereotyping seems especially important to understand because there is some evidence that minority children (particularly black girls) have high occupational aspirations while as adults they generally hold low-status occupations. An understanding of the development of ethnic stereotyping of occupations by whites, as well as by nonwhites might help us to pinpoint where things go wrong for minority children. Right now, however, we do not know much about the pattern of development of career awareness for any group.

The developmental course of career awareness

One can make the reasonable assumption that information about occupational behavior, about its antecedents and social consequences, and about the self increases as one matures, but we only know a little more about the development course of career awareness than that which we have just been willing to assume.

We have already reviewed evidence that children's awareness of a variety of careers, of the skills required by different occupations, and of the importance of occupations in defining adult roles increases during the early years (see page   ), and it is clear that young children's understanding of the social status hierarchy of occupations and of which occupations men and women are likely to hold in the United States is sufficiently great that little change can occur from early childhood on (see page   ). Unfortunately there is no evidence that, as children mature, they substantially correct their early stereotypes about careers. During adolescence, they do of course refine their occupational choices, and some change may occur in the aspirations of black children as they increasingly encounter the social realities of limited opportunity and discrimination. Decisions often, however, remain culturally-stereotyped, with original choices that were "sex-appropriate" or made by females changing less than those that were "sex-inappropriate" or made by males (*Carmody, Fenske* and *Scott,* 1972; *Rosenberg,* 1957; *Schmidt* and *Rothney,* 1955). These preliminary observations are about all we know at present about the course of development of career awareness from early childhood through adolescence. Because of this, we obviously know little about the stability of career awareness from childhood on.

There is, however, some evidence about stability during adolescence and early adulthood, but one immediately encounters the problem of defining which aspect of career awareness one is interested in: occupational choice *per se,* occupational values, level of occupational aspiration, or endorsement of occupational role assignments which are stereotyped by sex or ethnicity. Not all these aspects have been examined during adolescence and early adulthood, but there is some information worth recounting here.

The career plans of college and high school students seem relatively unstable. *Rosenberg* (1957) reports that 60 % of college students change their occupational plans at least once while at college. More recently, *Baird* (1973) found no significant correlation between the plans reported by students in their freshman and senior years, a finding that held true for males, females, blacks, whites, and students at high and low socioeconomic levels. *Schmidt* and *Rothney* (1957), *Carmody, Fenske,* and *Scott* (1972), and others describe similar or even greater instability of career choice by high school students.

On the other hand, the occupational value hierarchies of adolescent males do not change too much during the last four years of secondary schooling. *Montesano* and *Geist* (1964) report a rank order correlation of .82 in the saliency of seven occupational values held by boys tested in ninth and again in twelfth grades. *Gribbons* and *Lohnes* (1965) report a rank order correlation of .68 between the occupational values expressed by boys in the eighth grade and again in the twelfth grade. The rank order correlations from eighth to tenth grades and tenth to twelfth grades were .84 and .50 respectively. For girls the rank order correlations for occupational values were .95 from eight to tenth grade, .52 from tenth to twelfth grade, and .46 from eighth to twelfth grade. As we reported before, early concepts of occupational prestige and culturally-stereotyped occupational role assignments persist into adulthood. Indeed, early occupational choices which conform to cultural definitions of sex-appropriate employment are more stable than those which do not conform.

Although there is no direct evidence on the stability of career choices made before high school or college, these decisions surely must be at least as unstable as those made later. If our argument for the value of early career awareness were to rest upon the predictiveness of early career choices to later employment, little support could be mustered. However, our argument rests upon the opposite contention, that the better our efforts of creating early career awareness, the lower the predictiveness of early career choice to later success because children would be considering a greater range of career options. At present we know little about the developmental course of career awareness and its predictiveness for occupational choice, and we believe such information ought to be gathered. At the same time we ought to learn more about factors which influence early career awareness and later career choice.

Early influences on career awareness

Such evidence on the factors influencing the early development of career-related information and attitudes is unfortunately scarce. We can learn something from studies of the effects of viewing entertainment television and from evaluations of career education curricula. In addition, suggestions of avenues which might be pursued can be derived from studies of the career choices of adolescents and young adults. We begin this section with a review of these studies of external influences on the career choices of adolescents, then move to a review of the external influences of entertainment television and career education curricula on young children's career-related information and attitudes and conclude with some information on internal influences on career awareness.

External influences on career choice

Most adolescents and young adults list their parents (usually the same-sex parent) as most responsible for their career choices (*Jensen* and *Kirchner*, 1955; *Pallone, Hurley* and *Rickard*, 1973; *Pallone, Rickard* and *Hurley*, 1970; *Peters*, 1941; *Steinke* and *Kaczkowski*, 1961). The second source perceived as most responsible is usually someone holding the specific occupation the respondent has chosen (*Pallone, Rickard* and *Hurley*, 1970). All of these studies point to the retrospective ascription of potency to personally-known occupational models.

Several other studies of adolescents describe parent-child relationships and family structures as they relate to sex differences in differential motivation for occupational mobility (*Douvan* and *Adelson*, 1966; *Dynes, Clarke* and *Dinitz*, 1956; *Rosen*, 1956). These analyses point to the role of the family in creating substantial differences between adolescent boys and girls in the degree of autonomy, independence, assertiveness, and self-regulation. In all these areas related to occupational mobility, girls show weaker motivation. For younger children, similar differences in motivation between boys and girls have been described (e.g., *Lesser*, 1973; *Maccoby*, 1966; *Maccoby* and *Jacklin*, 1974; *Mischel*, 1970), but the relationship of these earlier differences to career performance has not been tested.

We have come to accept the peer group as the most salient influence upon the adolescent, operating as a "counterculture" that ignores, resists, or opposes the influence of adults. Surely, the adolescent's peer group does play a central role in matters of taste, dress, leisure activities, and certain social values. However, peers are far less influential than parents and other adults in determining long-range goals such as occupational choice and educational plans, and the influence that peers do exercise more often supports the attitudes of adults instead of opposing them (*Douvan* and *Adelson*, 1966; *Kandel* and *Lesser*, 1972). These findings hold true for both boys and girls.

If peers are less influential than parents and adult models, other potential sources of career direction are even less prominent than peers. Schools, teachers, guidance counselors, books and catalogues are rarely cited as influential by adolescents and adults. Schools and teachers surely play important roles in providing training for careers, but adolescents generally do not perceive them as important to their career choices.

Most of the studies of external influences upon career choice study them in isolation from each other. Rarely are the family, peers, schools, and teachers, and the media examined in combination. In addition, most studies are retrospective and use the student as his or her own informant. While information obtained in these ways may be useful, one cannot be confident that the respondent has been accurate in assessing sources of influence, especially when the report is obtained long after the fact. A few studies (e.g., *Jensen* and *Kirchner*, 1955; *Kandel* and *Lesser*, 1972) examine the concordance between parents' occupations and those selected by adolescents at the time their choices are being made. In these studies, workers are likely to have occupations similar to those of their same-sex parents or else a step above them in the status hierarchy, evidence which could be construed as confirming the respondents' own estimates that it was their parents who influenced their career choices. Still it is desirable to plan studies which utilize more experimental and observational procedures and less retrospective techniques. There have not been many such studies, although the few evaluations of intervention programs that we will describe do provide relevant information.

External influences on career information

Given the highly visible occupations which young children suggest they wish to be when they grow up, we can assume that much of their early information about careers comes from exposure to these careers within the community and the mass media. For instance, in a sample of mostly white eighth, ninth and tenth grade boys and girls, 89–97 % of them mentioned television as a source of information about each of six occupations, while 7–35 % mentioned print media, and 6–73 % mentioned other persons (*Jeffries-Fox* and *Signorielli,* 1979). In other work, at least a third of both black and white fourth, fifth, sixth, and eighth grade boys and girls reported that most of their information "about the jobs men and women have" and about "police, doctors, secretaries, nurses" comes from television (*Atkin, Greenberg,* and *McDermott,* 1979). A majority of both the blacks and whites also believed that the jobs they saw men and women performing on television were like those in real life (*Atkin, Greenberg,* and

McDermott, 1979). Both studies indicate that children believe they learn a great deal about occupations from television with encounters, with other people and reading perceived to be less prominent sources of information.

While self reports about sources of information can be inaccurate, it would not be surprising to find that television was in fact a major source of career information for young children. In an incidental manner it provides a great deal of occupational information. Unfortunately much of it is also superficial and misleading (*DeFleur* and *DeFleur,* 1967). For example, lawyers often are portrayed as clever users of legal tricks, police officers often are seen as hardened and unfeeling. Still, television provides "information" to children. Evaluations of Sesame Street segments on careers indicate that preschoolers can learn the names, activities, and accoutrements of occupations from it (*Bogatz* and *Ball,* 1971). Evaluations of other television series and of instructional units also indicate that minority and majority children from preschool through the sixth grade can gain information about occupations from them (*Bernabei* and *Case,* 1972; *Graves* and *Nelson-Shapiro,* 1974; *Harkness,* 1973).

External influences on career attitudes

Except for a few studies of the effects of television programs and of career education curricula, which we will discuss in a moment, only one study addresses the impact of external sources on career attitudes. It is the *Cordua, McGraw,* and *Drabman* (1979) study described earlier. They report that children in a school where both male and female nurses had visited had much less difficulty identifying the male nurse in the two videotapes in which he appeared. They also report that for the videotape of a female doctor and a male nurse the children of working mothers were much more likely to identify the characters correctly. Thus, there is some indication – as one would expect – that personal experiences with workers will influence young children's career attitudes.

Entertainment television and career education curricula can also influence their attitudes. Three- to six-year-olds who are heavy viewers of television are more likely than light viewers to stereotype occupations on the basis of sex (*Beuf,* 1974). Even adults who are heavy viewers, as compared to light viewers, believe that more men have law enforcement jobs, that more white and nonwhite Americans are employed in professional and managerial occupations, and that more Americans are employed as professional athletes, entertainers, and artists (*Gerbner* and *Gross,* 1973). While neither of these studies permits inferences about the direction of effects, most people assume that it is television viewing which contributes to the development of these stereotypes rather than vice versa. Two studies have, in fact, demonstrated that television commercials which portray women in nontraditional occupational roles can influence children's beliefs about the division of labor between the sexes (*Atkin*, 1975; *Pingree*, 1975) and the influence was stronger when children were led to believe that the commercials represented real women (*Pingree*, 1975).

It is not at all surprising to find that heavier viewers of American television have more stereotyped opinions about the occupational roles of men and women and the various ethnic groups, since every category of television programming which has been examined presents them in stereotyped occupational roles (*Tuchman, Daniels,* and *Benét,* 1978; *U.S. Commission on Civil Rights,* 1977, 1979). Women have been found to be much less frequently employed outside the home in children's programming (*Ormiston* and *Williams,* 1973), commercials (*Courtney* and *Whipple,* 1974), prime-time programming (*Tedesco,* 1974), and daytime soap operas (*Downing,* 1974). Blacks have been found to be much less frequently employed than whites in children's programming (*Mendelson* and *Young,* 1972; *Ormiston* and *Williams,* 1973). Other minority groups are so infrequently presented that one cannot characterize their employment patterns. Taking only those men and women, or whites and nonwhites, who are employed outside the home, white males are more likely to occupy higher status occupations than white women or minorities of either sex. The few times where this is not true, the number of employed women or minorities is so small that the patterns of occupational attainment can be skewed by changes in the occupations of only one or two characters.

Evaluations of three sets of career education materials indicate that curricula can influence attitudes. This includes videotapes of five different occupations designed to produce "a more positive attitude about work" among sixth graders (*Bernabei* and *Case,* 1972), six career education lessons which increased attitudes (occupational prestige, distaste for some occupations, and understanding of the nature of one's own occupational choice) in fourth-through-sixth grade blacks and whites (*Harkness,* 1973), and books about working women which affected kindergarteners' perceptions of the jobs women could do (*Barclay,* 1974).

Most career awareness curricula unfortunately do not challenge traditional views of the occupational roles of men and women, whites and minorities (*Leifer* and *Lesser,* 1976). The clearest attention to stereotyping by sex or ethnicity occurs in three sets of inserts for public or commercial television programs for children between the ages of three and eight (*Kingdom of Could Be You, Sesame*

Street, and *Vegetable Soup*) and in a new series, *Freestyle,* for children in the later grades of elementary school (*Williams,* 1979). Other curricula, all aimed at children who are at least five years old, do not explicitly address the issue of occupational stereotyping and, as far as one can determine, do not do so implicitly either. This means that these external influencers of career attitudes do not counter the stereotypes young white and black children already hold about the occupations which are appropriate for white (or black) men and women. Children are then exposed to career information – much like that in the rest of their world – which either ignores women and minorities or which places them predominately in the lower status occupations.

Internal influences on career awareness

Among adolescents and young adults, the effect of personal characteristics upon career choice is well-documented. In an earlier section of this paper, these influences were discussed: preferences and interests; abilities and aptitudes; aspirations and expectations; motives and values; knowledge and experience with occupations; self-concept and sense of competence.

Self-concept and sense of competence are, of course, of primary importance in career choice. To the extent that self-concept is stereotyped by one's sex or race, one's occupational orientation may be similarly stereotyped. Where this occurs, the study of career development dovetails with the development of sex-roles and race-roles. Alleviating stereotyping in one should be reflected in less stereotyping in the others. Thus, any understanding of the development of career orientations must contain an analysis of sex-role and race-role development. These aspects of self-concept may contribute heavily to attitudinal influences on occupational aspiration and achievement.

Because there are several clear examples of relationships between careers and the development of sex-role attitudes, we will focus on these to the exclusion of race-role attitudes for the rest of this section. It is not our intention here to document all the ways in which self-concept and personality may influence career awareness; to do so for each sex within each ethnic group would take much more time and space than we have. Rather, we wish to point out the saliency that variables, other than those generally classed under career development, may have and we can do that reasonably well with the example of sex-role attitudes.

For men, strong achievement motivation is associated with occupational performance and mobility; one component of achievement motivation in particular, fear of failure, is a strong deterrent to occupational success for men (*Crok-kett*, 1973; *Lipset* and *Bendix*, 1959; *McClelland* and *Steele*, 1973; *McClelland* and *Winter*, 1969; *Rosen*, 1956). For women, the burden of fearing failure is only one psychological deterrent to achievement. Fear of success is perhaps more pervasive and more crippling for them. This observation has a long history. Analyses by both *Freud* (1933) and *Mead* (1949) stating that competitive achievement becomes consciously or unconsciously equated with loss of femininity have been reconfirmed in recent studies of women (*Horner*, 1973; *Lesser*, 1973), although there are indications that black women show less fear of success than white women (*Weston* and *Mednick*, 1972).

There is little evidence that young girls fear success in the same way that women do (*Maccoby* and *Jacklin*, 1974), and there are indications that young girls are eager to compete and achieve when the tasks set for them are defined as neutral or feminine (*Stein, Pohly,* and *Mueller,* 1971). When tasks are defined as masculine (as most prestigious occupations and test stimuli have been), girls retreat to their "stereotypical" lack of motivation. Perhaps some of white women's fear of failure and success and low career aspirations arise from the fact that they will not compete in arenas they view as masculine. Unfortunately, there are no research signs as yet that the growing emphasis on women's rights has reduced women's fear of success, as it is traditionally measured. Any analysis of sex differences in career decisions must include the development of this element of self-concept in women: the motive not only to avoid failure, but success as well.

The connections between career and self-concept are different for boys and girls. Studying adolescents, *Douvan* and *Adelson* (1966) report that an essential ingredient in boys' self-concept comes from their search for a work identity. Boys' discussions of future plans reveal a consistent preoccupation with choosing and preparing for a future vocational role. When their opportunities for meaningful contact with occupational work are limited, great confusion results in their development of self-concept (*Goodman*, 1960). For adolescent girls, *Douvan* and *Adelson* report less personal investment in future work, ". . . a less differentiated picture of the world of work, a less discriminating view of the content of the particular job to which they aspire" (p. 36). When *Douvan* and *Adelson* grouped occupations according to the long-term commitment they require, only 10 % of adolescent girls want these jobs compared with 47 % of adolescent boys. The current movements for women's rights may be modifying this picture somewhat. Men and women in recent graduating classes at such universities as Harvard and Stanford are reported to aspire equally to the same professional careers. Even their professed interests in marriage and children are roughly equivalent. At Stanford, women have remained in graduate programs at the same rate men have since at least 1972 (*Carlsmith,* personal communication). While these changes have occurred among men and women in fairly unrepresentative environments, they at least indicate that such change is possible.

Barnett's (1973) study extends these connections among self-concept, sex-role, and careers, adding occupational prestige to the analysis. Boys and girls differ at every age from nine to seventeen, with the correlations between occupational prestige and preference being higher for boys than for girls. Conversely, for girls at every age the relationship between prestige and aversion is positive and stronger than for boys. These data point to early sex-related learning with regard to the attractiveness of prestigious occupations: boys learn to prefer them, girls learn to reject them. *Barnett* did not study the self-concepts of boys and girls directly, but her data clearly imply that girls consider themselves unworthy of prestigious occupations or consider these jobs inaccessible to them.

Turner's theory (1964) places these observations in a broader perspective. He concludes from his data that girls' self-concepts derive from the fact that they attain success largely by being chosen by others rather than through their own direct pursuit of success. In contrast, boys learn that they must take an active role in gaining acceptance and success, must be self-reliant and self-regulating, and must learn to delay gratification in order to achieve lasting success.

These ideas about sex-differences in self-concept and their implications for career development may sound old-fashioned and outmoded by the current efforts of women to gain equal rights and equal treatment. Although our optimism must lead us to hope that significant changes are occurring in both self-concepts and career opportunities of women, no direct evidence has accumulated yet to support that optimism. Until such evidence appears, we must assume that other efforts, along with the women's and civil-rights movements, must be made to redress the gross inequities based on sex. We believe that similar assertions can be made about inequities based on race, but there is much less available data to support or refute them now.

Combinations of influence

The studies which we have reviewed on the external and internal influences on career awareness and choice rarely consider combinations of factors which undoubtedly contribute to career development. Their objectives have been to assess the relative influence of each source and not to determine how the several sources reinforce or compete with each other. Family, schools and teachers, peers, adult models, the mass media, and personal characteristics are each considered in isolation from the other (e.g., *Coleman,* 1961). When more than one source is encompassed within a specific study (e.g., *Kandel* and *Lesser,* 1972), it is to estimate their comparative importance in influencing occupational choice.

There is value in knowing how each source of influence operates. For example, how do different families affect the career decisions of their children? Or, how do sex-role attitudes contribute to career choice? But we must begin to discover how various influences combine to build career awareness. Surely the child experiences these influences in combination, not singly, and their interaction must be considered in any effort to assist career choice.

While we know very little about the effects of combinations of influence upon the development of career awareness, we can predict that they are particularly important. For instance, for children who are exposed to many adult occupational role models, additional information from teachers, books, and television may be easily accepted and integrated into their existing framework of occupations. On the other hand, those children who have less immediate experience with adult workers may find it difficult to accept or utilize information that comes from these secondary sources. They will need a combination of live role models, instruction, work experience, and mediated models to form an adequate impression of the range of occupations available to them. For the young child in particular, it is our contention that the particular combination of family, the mass media, the school and the child's developing self-concept will exert the most powerful influence on career awareness.

Conclusion

The causes of the unequal occupational status of women and minorities are deep and pervasive. Simply understanding and improving the early forms of career awareness in young children, as we have recommended, may seem too weak and too naive an expedient by itself to overcome the massive barriers to equality for women and minorities. However, suppose the following assertions are true:

- Young children do develop concepts about careers very early in their lives, but because their information and experience are fragmentary, their concepts are narrow and stereotypic.

- Once early stereotypes are formed and no concerted effort is made to counter them, they persist into adolescence and young adulthood with only superficial improvements and expansions based on a child's personal experiences with employed persons.
- The majority of adolescents and young adults thus make career decisions while relatively uninformed of the range and variety of opportunities available to them and of the exact nature of the occupations within that range.

If these conditions are indeed pervasive, we may be overlooking a deceptively direct avenue for expanding occupational opportunities for women and minorities, one that can never reverse the basic political and economic causes of inequality but can provide a fuller view of options to those who need that perspective most.

Suppose we understood more about the early development of concepts about careers and could find ways to expand them and correct misleading stereotypes at early ages. Suppose that this expanded awareness could be carried forward and built upon into adolescence and young adulthood so that when career decisions are made, they are based on a wider vision of careers that exist now or may emerge in the future, especially for women and minorities. Against the powerful political and economic obstacles that block occupational equality for women and minorities, would this understanding of the early development of career awareness really matter? Until we try this route, it is impossible to tell. However, the following assumptions seem plausible: for children, the present invisibility of occupations imposes important restrictions on career choice; these restrictions operate with special force for girls and minorities; it is presently within our means to begin correcting these conditions.

The mass media, particularly television and film, provide us with some of the easiest opportunities to guarantee that our children see men and women of all ethnic groups in a wide range of occupations. They alone can reliably provide concrete models of people who do not hold traditional occupations. Yet entertainment television is presently one of the most powerful conveyors of sex and race stereotypes (cf., *U.S. Commission on Civil Rights,* 1977, 1979). Many of the television curricula do not actively counter stereotypes (*Leifer* and *Lesser,* 1976), and the television industry itself displays persisting traditional patterns in employment of women and minorities (*U.S. Commission on Civil Rights,* 1977, 1979). For example, 1974 employment figures compiled by the Federal Communications Commission show that only 12 % of the full-time work force are from minorities in both commercial and non-commercial stations, while women constitute only 24 % of the full-time workers in commercial stations and 31 % in non-commercial stations. Among television writers, less than 10 % are women. We do not contend that only women and minority writers and producers can produce non-sexist and non-racist material, but surely they must be enlisted in greater numbers if the mass media are to fulfill their potential to dispel the stereotypes based upon sex and race.

Some would ask: Why arouse expectations that our institutions have no intention of meeting? We will not argue that our institutions show any visible readiness to meet the career aspirations of women and minorities. Neither are we willing to believe, however, that perpetuating ignorance and obliviousness is a reasonable course, even for the purpose of avoiding disappointment. Although it may be wise to keep this risk in mind, society's stereotypes will not change until individuals' attitudes do, and *vice versa*. For it is, after all, individuals who form and direct our society. If any real progress is to occur, efforts must be made at both the individual and institutional levels. They are mutually reinforcing and mutually constraining.

Footnotes

[1] The original report was prepared while Aimee *Dorr* was on the faculty of the Harvard University Graduate School of Education with Gerald S. *Lesser*. She has since moved to the University of Southern California, where the revised chapter was prepared. All correspondence should be addressed to Aimee Dorr, Annenberg School of Communications, University of Southern California, University Park, Los Angeles, California 90007.

[2] Because *Kirchner* and *Vondracek* report occupational aspirations in a mixed list of specific occupations *and* occupational types, an exact count of the number of specific occupations is not possible.

References

Antonovsky, A.: Aspirations, class and racial-ethnic membership. In: Journal of Negro Education, 36/1967/–, pp. 385 – 393.

Atkin, Charles K.: The effects of television advertising on children. Second year experimental evidence. Unpublished manuscript. Michigan State University 1975.

Atkin, Charles K.; Greenberg, Bradley; McDermott, S.: Race and social role learning from television. In: Dordick, H.S. (ed.): Proceedings of the sixth Annual Telecommunications Policy Research Conference. Lexington, Mass.: Lexington Books 1979.

Baird, Leonard; Clark, Mary Jo; Hartnett, Rodney T.: The graduates. A report on the plans and characteristics of college seniors. Princeton, N.J.: Educational Testing Service 1973. VII, 210 p.

Barclay, L.K.: The emergence of vocational expectations in preschool children. In: Journal of Vocational Behavior, 4/1974/–, pp. 1 – 14.

Bardwick, Judith M.: Psychology of women. A study of bio-cultural conflicts. New York: Harper & Row 1971. VII, 242 p.

Barnett, R.C.: The relationship between occupational prestige. A study of sex differences and age trends. Paper presented at Meeting of the American Psychological Association, Montreal, August 1973. N.p.: n.pr. 1973.

Barnett, R.C.; Baruch, G.: Occupational and educational aspirations and expectations. A review of empirical literature. N.p.: n.pr. 1973.

Baugham, Emmet Earl; Dahlstrom, W. Grant: Negro and white children. A psychological study in the rural South. New York: Academic Press 1968. XXIII, 572 p.

Baumrind, D.: From each according to her ability. In: School Review, 80/1972/–, pp. 161 – 197.

Bernabei, R.; Case, J.: Career awareness/job orientation via taped television programs. Unpublished manuscript. Hazelton Pennsylvania School District 1972.

Beuf, A.: Doctor, lawyer, household drudge. In: Journal of Communication, 24/1974/–, pp. 142 – 145.

Bogatz, Gerry Ann; Ball, Samuel: The second year of Sesame Street. A continuing evaluation, vol. 1 – 2. A report to the Children's Television Workshop. Princeton, N.J.: Educational Testing Service 1971.

Boyd, G.F.: The levels of aspiration of white and Negro children in a nonsegregated elementary school. In: Journal of Social Psychology, 36/1952/–, pp. 191 – 196.

Boynton, P.: The vocational preferences of school children. In: Journal of Genetic Psychology, 49/1936/–, pp. 411 – 425.

Caplow, Theodore: The sociology of work. Minneapolis: Univ. of Minnesota Press 1954. 330 p.

Carlsmith, J.M.: Personal communication. Stanford, Calif.: Stanford Univ. 1972.

Carmody, James Francis; Fenske, Robert Harland; Scott, C.S.: Changes in goals, plans and background characteristics of college-bound high school students. Iowa City, Iowa: American College Testing Program, Research and Development Division 1972. 31 p.

Clark, E.T.: Influence of sex and social class on occupational preference and perception. In: Personnel and Guidance Journal, 45/1967/–, pp. 440 – 444.

Clark, Edward T.: Culturally disadvantaged boys' and girls' aspirations to and knowledge of white-collar and professional occupations. In: Urban Education, 1/1965/3, pp. 164 – 174.

Cloward, R.A.; Jones, J.A.: Social class. Educational attitudes and participation. In: Passow, Harry A. (ed.): Education in depressed areas. New York: Columbia Univ. 1963.

Coleman, James Samuel: The adolescent society. The social life of the teenager and its impact on education. New York: Free Press of Glencoe 1961. XVI, 368 p.

Cordua, G.D.; McGraw, K.O.; Drabman, R.S.: Doctor or nurse. Children's perception of sex-typed occupations. In: Child Development, 50/1979/–, pp. 590 – 593.

Courtney, A.E.; Whipple, T.W.: Women in TV commercials. In: Journal of Communication, 24/1974/–, pp. 110 – 118.

Creason, F.; Schilson, D.L.: Occupational concerns of sixth grade children. In: Vocational Guidance Quarterly, 18/1970/–, pp. 219 – 224.

Crockett, H.J.: The achievement motive and differential occupational mobility in the United States. In: McClelland, David Clarence (eds.) et al.: Human motivation. A book of readings. Morristown, N.J.: General Learning Press 1973.

Crooks, R.C.: The effects of an interracial preschool program upon racial preference, knowledge of racial differences and racial identification. In: Journal of Social Issues, 27/1971/–, pp. 213 – 235.

Davis, D.A.; Hagan, N.; Strouf, J.: Occupational choice of twelve-year-olds. In: Personnel and Guidance Journal, 40/1962/–, pp. 628 – 629.

DeFleur, M.L.: Children's knowledge of occupational roles and prestige. Preliminary report. In: Psychological Reports, 13/1963/–, pp. 760 – 761.

DeFleur, M.L.; DeFleur, L.B.: The relative contribution of television as a learning source for children's occupational knowledge. In: American Sociological Review, 32/1967/–, pp. 777 – 789.

Deutsch, M.: Race and social class as separate factors related to social environment. In: American Journal of Sociology, 70/1965/–, p. 474.

Deutsch, Martin: Minority group and class status as related to social and personality factors in scholastic achievement. Ithaca, N.Y.: Society for Applied Anthropology 1960. 32 p.

Douvan, Elizabeth Ann Malcolm; Adelson, Joseph: The adolescent experience. New York: Wiley 1966. XII, 471 p.

Downing, M.: Heroine of the daytime serial. In: Journal of Communication, 24/1974/–, pp. 130 – 137.

Dynes, R.R.; Clarke, A.C.; Dinitz, S.: Levels of occupational aspiration. Some aspects of family experience as a variable. In: American Sociological Review, 21/1956/–, pp. 212 – 215.

Fine, S.A.; Heinz, C.A.: The estimates of worker trait requirements for 4,000 jobs. In: Personnel and Guidance Journal, 36/1957/–, pp. 168 – 174.

Fine, S.A.; Heinz, C.A.: The functional occupational classification structure. In: Personnel and Guidance Journal, 37/1958/–, pp. 180 – 192.

Freud, Sigmund: The psychology of women. In: Freud, Sigmund: New introductory lectures in psychoanalysis. New York: Horton 1933.

Garrett, C.S.; Ein, P.L.; Tremaine, L.: The development of gender stereotyping of adult occupations in elementary school children. In: Child Development, 48/1977/–, pp. 507 – 512.

Gerbner, G.; Gross, L.: Abstract from cultural indicators. The social reality of television drama. Proposal for the renewal of a research grant. Philadelphia, Pa.: Annenberg School of Communication, Univ. of Pennsylvania 1973.

Ginzberg, Eli (coll.); *Ginsburg, S.W.* (coll.); *Axelrad, S.* (coll.) et al.: Occupational choice. An approach to a general theory. New York: Columbia Univ. Press 1951. VIII, 271 p.

Goldblatt, H.; Tyson, C.: Some self-perceptions and teacher evaluations of Puerto Rican, Negro, and white pupils in 4th, 5th, and 6th grades (P.S. 198 M). New York: New York City Commission on Human Rights 1962.

Goodman, Mary Ellen: Race awareness in young children. Rev. ed. New York: Collier Books 1964. 351 p.

Goodman, Paul S.: Growing up absurd. New York: Random House 1960. 296 p.

Goodson, S.: Children talk about work. In: Personnel and Guidance Journal 49/1970/–, pp. 131 – 136.

Graves, S.B.; Nelson-Shapiro, B.: Formative research report. Cambridge, Mass.: Harvard Univ. 1974.

Gray, S.: The vocational preferences of Negro school children. In: Journal of Genetic Psychology, 64/1944/–, pp. 239 – 247.

Gribbons, W.D.; Lohnes, P.R.: Shifts in adolescents' vocational values. In: Personnel and Guidance Journal, 44/1965/–, pp. 248 – 252.

Gump, J.P.; Rivers, L.W.: The consideration of race in efforts to end sex bias. Washington, D.C.: National Institute of Education 1973.

Gurin, Patricia; Katz, Daniel: Motivation and aspiration in the Negro college. Ann Arbor, Mich.: Survey Research Center, Institute for Social Research, Univ. of Michigan 1966. XVI, 346 p.

Hales, L.W.: Fenner, B.: Work values of fifth, eighth, and eleventh grade students. In: Vocational Guidance Quarterly, 20/1972/–, pp. 199 – 203.

Hansen, J.C.; Caulfield, T.J.: Parent-child occupational concepts. In: Elementary School Guidance and Counseling, 3/1969/–, pp. 269 – 275.

Harkness, S.C.: The influence of vocational information on the career development of elementary school children. Paper presented at the Annual Meeting of AERA, New Orleans, La. February 1973. N.p.: n.pr. 1973.

Herriott, Robert E.; St. John, Nancy Hoyt: Social class and the urban school. The impact of pupil background on teachers and principals. New York: Wiley 1966. XVI, 289 p.

Hess, Robert D.; Torney, Judith V.: The development of political attitudes in children. Chicago: Aldine 1967. XVIII, 288 p.

Hill, Robert Bernard: The strengths of black families. New York: National Urban League 1971. Various pagings.

Hindelang, M.J.: Educational and occupational aspirations among Negro, Mexican-American, and White elementary school children. In: Journal of Negro Education, 39/1970–, pp. 351 – 353.

Holland, John L.: The psychology of vocational choice. A theory of personality types and environmental models. Waltham, Mass.: Blaisdell 1966. IX, 132 p.

Horner, M.S.: A psychological barrier to achievement in women. The motive to avoid success. In: McClelland, David Clarence (eds.) et al.: Human motivation. A book of readings. Morristown, N.J.: General Learning Press 1973.

Hyman, Herbert Hiram: Political socialization. A study in the psychology of political behavior. Glencoe, Ill.: Free Press 1959. 175 p.

Jeffries-Fox, S.; Signorielli, N.: Television and children's conceptions of occupations. In: Dordick, H.S. (ed.): Proceedings of the sixth Annual Telecommunications Policy Research Conference. Lexington, Mass.: Lexington Books 1979.

Jencks, Christopher: Inequality. A reassessment of the effect of family and schooling in America. New York: Basic Books 1972. XII, 399 p.

Jensen, P.G.; Kirchner, W.K.: A national answer to the question, "Do sons follow their fathers' occupations?" In: Journal of Applied Psychology, 39/1955/–, pp. 419 – 421.

Kandel, Denis Bystryn; Lesser, Gerald S.: Youth in two worlds. United States and Denmark. San Francisco: Jossey-Bass 1972. 217 p.

Kirchner, E.P.; Vondracek, S.I.: What do you want to be when you grow up? Vocational choice in children aged three to six. Paper presented at the Society for Research in Child Development, Philadelphia, March 1973. N.p.: n. pr. 1973.

Kleinke, C.L.; Nicholson, T.A.: Black and white children's awareness of de facto race and sex differences. In: Developmental Psychology, 15/1979/–, pp. 84 – 86.

Kohlberg, L.: A cognitive-developmental analysis of children's sex-role concepts and attitudes. In: Maccoby, Eleanor E. (ed.): The development of sex differences. Stanford, Calif.: Stanford Univ. Press 1966.

Kohlberg, L.: Stage and sequence. The cognitive-developmental approach to socialization. In Goslin, David A. (ed.): Handbook of socialization theory and research. Chicago: Rand McNally 1969.

Koslin, S.C. et al.: Quasi-designed and structured measure of school-children's racial preferences. Washington, D.C.: American Psychological Association 1969.

Kreps, Juanita Morris: Sex in the marketplace. American women at work. Baltimore: Hopkins 1971. X, 117 p.

Kuvlesky, W.P.; Thomas, K.A.: Social ambitions of Negro boys and girls from a metropolitan ghetto. In: Journal of Vocational Behavior, 1/1971/–, pp. 177 - 187.

Lee, P.C.; Gropper, N.B.: Sex-role culture and educational practice. In: Harvard Educational Review, 44/1974/–, pp. 369 – 410.

Lefebvre, A.; Bohn, M.J.: Occupational prestige as seen by disadvantaged black children. In: Developmental Psychology, 4/1971/–, pp. 173 – 177.

Leifer, Aimée Dorr; Lesser, Gerald S.: The development of career awareness in young children. Unpublished manuscript. Cambridge, Mass.: Harvard University 1976. 72 p.

Lesser, G.S.: Achievement motivation in women. In: McClelland, David Clarence (eds.) et al.: Human motivation. A book of readings. Morristown, N.J.: General Learning Press 1973.

Lipset, Seymour Marlen; Bendix, Reinhard: Social mobility in industrial society. Berkeley: Univ. of California Press 1959. XXI, 309 p.

Looft, W.R.: Sex differences in the expression of vocational aspirations by elementary school children. In: Developmental Psychology, 5/1971/–, p. 366.

Maccoby, Eleanor E. (ed.): The development of sex differences. Stanford. Calif.: Stanford Univ. Press 1966. 351 p.

Maccoby, Eleanor E.; Jacklin, Carol Nagy: The psychology of sex differences. Stanford, Calif.: Stanford Univ. Press 1974. XIII, 634 p.

McCandless, B.R.: Childhood socialization. In: Goslin, David A. (ed.): Handbook of socialization theory and research. Chicago: Rand McNally 1969.

McClelland, David Clarence; Steele, Robert C.: Human motivation. A book of readings. Morristown, N.J.: General Learning Press 1973. X, 510 p.

McClelland, David Clarence; Winter, David G.: Motivating economic achievement. New York: Free Press 1969. XXII, 409 p.

Mead, Margaret: Male and female. New York: Morrow 1949. XII, 477 p.

Mendelson, Gilbert; Young, Morissa: Network children's programming. A content analysis of black and minority treatment on children's television. Prepared for Action for Children's Television. Washington, D.C.: Black Efforts for Soul in Television 1972. 20 p.

Miller, Delbert Charles; Form, William H.: Industrial sociology. An introduction to the sociology of work relations. New York: Harper 1951. XI, 896 p.

Mischel, W.: Sex-typing and socialization. In: Mussen, Paul H. (ed.): Manual of child psychology, vol. 2. New York: Wiley 1970.

Montemayor, R.; Eisen, M.: The development of self-conceptions from childhood to adolescence. In: Developmental Psychology, 13/1977/–, pp. 314 – 319.

Montesano, N.; Geist, H.: Differences in occupational choice between ninth and twelfth grade boys. In: Personnel and Guidance Journal, 43/1964/–, pp. 150 – 154.

Monthly Labor Review, January 1975.

Morland, J.K.: Racial acceptance and preference of nursery school children in a southern city. In: Merrill-Palmer Quarterly, 8/1962/–, pp. 217 – 280.

Morland, J.K.: Racial attitudes in school children. From kindergarten through high school. A final report. Lynchburg, Va.: Randolph Macon College 1972.

Mussen, Paul H.: Early sex-role development: In: Goslin, David A. (ed.): Handbook of socialization theory and research. Chicago: Rand McNally 1969.

Nelson, J.C.: Interests of disadvantaged and advantaged Negro and White first graders. In: Journal of Negro Education, 37/11968/–, p. 168 – 173.

Nelson, R.C.: Knowledge and interests concerning sixteen occupations among elementary and secondary school students. In: Educational and Psychological Measurement, 23/1963/–, pp. 741 – 754.

O'Hara, R.P.: The roots of careers. In: Elementary School Journal, 62/1962/–, pp. 277 – 280.

Ormiston, L.H.; Williams, S.: Saturday children's programming in San Francisco, California. An analysis of the presentation of racial and cultural groups on three network affiliated San Francisco television stations. San Francisco: Committee on Children's TV 1973.

Osipow, S.H.; Ashby, J.D.; Wall, H.W.: Personality types and vocational choice. A test of Holland's theory, In: Personnel and Guidance Journal, 45/1966/–, pp. 37 – 42.

Pallone, N.J.; Hurley, R.B.; Rickard, F.S.: Further data on key influencers of occupational expectations among minority youth. In: Journal of Counseling Psychology, 20/1973/–, pp. 484 – 486.

Pallone, N.J.; Rickard, F.S.; Hurley, R.B.: Key influencers of occupational preference among black youths. In: Journal of Counseling Psychology, 17/1970/–, pp. 498 – 501.

Peters, E.F.: Factors which contribute to youth's vocational choice. In: Journal of Applied Psychology, 25/1941/–, pp. 428 - 430.

Pingree, S.: A developmental study of the attitudinal effects of nonsexist television commercials under varied conditions of perceived reality. Stanford, Calif., Stanford Univ., diss. 1975.

Porter, Judith D.R.: Black child, white child. The development of racial attitudes. Cambridge, Mass.: Harvard Univ. Press 1971. XI, 278 p.

Reiss, A.J.; Rhodes, 4.L.: Are educational norms and goals of conforming, truant, and delinquent adolescents influenced by group position in American society? In: Journal of Negro Education, 28/1959/–, pp. 252 – 267.

Roe, Anne: The psychology of occupations. New York: Wiley 1956. 340 p.

Rosen, B.C.: The achievement syndrome. In: American Sociological Review, 21/1956/–, pp. 203 – 211.

Rosenberg, Morris: Occupations and values. Glencoe, Ill.: Free Press 1957. 158 p.

Scanzoni, John H.: The black family in modern society. Boston: Allyn and Bacon 1971. X, 353 p.

Schlossberg, N.K.; Goodman, J.: A woman's place. Children's sex stereotypes of occupations. In: Vocational Guidance Quarterly, 20/1972/–, pp. 266 – 270.

Schmidt, J.L.; Rothney, J.W.M.: Variability of vocational choices of high school students. In: Personnel and Guidance Journal, 34/1955/–, pp. 142 – 146.

Siegel, C.L.F.: Sex differences in the occupational choices of second graders. In: Journal of Vocational Behavior, 3/1973/–, pp. 15 – 19.

Simmons, D.: Children's rankings of occupational prestige. In: Personnel und Guidance Journal, 41/1962/–, pp. 332 – 335.

Simmons, R.G.; Rosenberg, M.: Functions of children's perceptions of the stratification system. In: American Sociological Review, 36/1971/–, pp. 235 – 249.

Snelbecker, G.F.; Arffa, M.S.: An evaluation of an integrated summer school program. Brockton, Mass.: Veterans Administration Hospital 1966.

Stein, A.H.; Pohly, S.R.; Mueller, E.: The influence of masculine, feminine and neutral tasks on children's achievement behavior, expectancies of success, and attainment values. In: Child Development, 42/1971/–, pp. 195 – 208.

Steinke, B.K.; Kaczkowski, H.R.: Parents' influence on the occupational choices of 9th grade girls. In: Vocational Guidance Quarterly, 9/1961/–, pp. 101 – 103.

Stockin, B.C.: A test of Holland's occupational level formulation. In: Personnel and Guidance Journal, 42/1964/–, pp. 599 – 602.

Super, Donald Edwin: The psychology of careers. An introduction to vocational development. New York: Harper 1957. 362 p.

Sutton-Smith, Brian: The folkgames of children. Published for the American Folklore Society. Austin, Texas: Univ. of Texas Press 1972. XVI, 559 p.

Tedesco, N.S.: Patterns in prime time. In: Journal of Communication, 24/1974/–, pp. 119 – 124.

Tiedemann, David V.; O'Hara, Robert P.: Career development. Choice and adjustment. Differentiation and integration in career development. New York: College Entrance Examination Board 1963. VII, 108 p.

Tuchman, Gaye (ed.); *Daniels, Arlene Kaplan* (ed.); *Benét, James* (ed.): Hearth and home. Images of women in the mass media. New York: Oxford Univ. Press 1978. XI, 333 p.

Turner, Ralph H.: The social context of ambition. San Francisco: Chandler 1964. XV, 269 p.

United States, Commission on Civil Rights (ed.): Window dressing on the set. Women and minorities in television. A report. Washington, D.C.: U.S. Government Printing Office 1977. IX, 181 p.

United States, Commission on Civil Rights (ed.): Window dressing on the set. An update. Washington, D.C.: U.S. Government Printing Office 1979.

United States, Employment Service, Division of Occupational Analysis (ed.): Dictionary of occupational titles. 2nd ed. Washington, D.C.: U.S. Government Printing Office 1949. 194 p.

United States, Department of Labor, Women's Bureau (ed.): Handbook of women workers, 1969. Washington D.C.: U.S. Government Printing Office 1970.

Waldman, E.; McEaddy, B.J.: Where women work. An analysis by industry and occupation. In: Monthly Labor Review, 97/1974/–, pp. 3 – 13.

Weinstein, E.A.: Children's conceptions of occupational stratification. In: Sociology and Social Research, 42/1958/–, pp. 278 – 284.

Weston, P.J.; Mednick, M.T.: Race, social class and motive to avoid success. In: Bardwick, Judith M. (ed.): Readings on the psychology of women. New York: Harper & Row 1972.

Williams, F.: "Freestyle". Using television to combat sex-role stereotyping in children. In: Dordick, H.S. (ed.): Proceedings of the sixth Annual Telecommunications Policy Research Conference. Lexington, Mass.: Lexington Books 1979.

Wright, D.E. et al.: Ambitions and opportunities for social mobility and their consequences for Mexican Americans as compared with other youth. Washington, D.C.: Department of Agriculture 1972.

Wylie, R.C.: Children's estimates of their schoolwork as a function of sex, race, and socioeconomic level. In: Journal of Personality, 31/1963/–, pp. 203 – 224.

Ellen Wartella

Children's impressions of television mothers*

One of the striking characteristics of American television is the degree to which it has presented stereotypical portrayals of women and other minority groups. Recently, the United States Civil Right Commission (1977, 1979) completed extensive reviews of the nature and extent of the limited kinds of portrayals of women on American television since the 1950's. Women have been systematically underrepresented in numbers on television, constituting somewhere between 25 and 30 % of all characters. Typically, women have been portrayed in a limited range of occupations, such as secretary, nurse and housewife. They tend to be young, attractive, generally passive and dominated by the males as opposed to dominating (*Tedesco,* 1974; *Lemon,* 1979; *Tuchman,* 1978; *Sternglanz* and *Serbin,* 1974). Overall, the limited range of occupations, personality traits, and acceptable behaviors shown to attach to women has led to considerable complaints of abusive stereotyping (U.S. Civil Rights Commission, 1977, 1979).

The sorts of social roles women characters are elaborating on television provide child viewers with models for their own behaviors and expectations about how these social roles are to be enacted. Since social roles are elaborated by specific characters engaging in a variety of social actions, it would be useful to examine how child viewers interpret these roles. Research focusing on children's interpretations and evaluations, or impressions of characters on television should lead to better understanding of children's social learning from the medium. Social role learning from television should include children's learning about the range of acceptable behaviors, attitudes and norms appropriate for various roles. Of particular interest here is children's learning about appropriate family roles and behaviors from family-oriented television programs. In recent years, American family relationships have been frequently depicted in both situation comedy formats and "family dramas". Children may acquire much socially important information about how families, particularly mothers, are supposed to behave by watching such programming.

* The study reported here was supported through a grant from the John and Mary Markle Foundation to Professors Daniel B. *Wackman* and W. Andrew *Collins,* University of Minnesota, entitled "Children's pro-social learning from family-oriented television."

In order to assess both the range of behaviors portrayed by television families and children's impressions of such characters, two types of data are examined here. A content analysis of nine family-oriented television shows was employed to describe the range of behaviors of mothers on American television during the 1975–76 television season. Secondly, children in second, fifth and eighth grades were surveyed about their impressions of several of these television mothers. These data are part of a larger study of children's social learning about television families reported elsewhere (*Wackman, Collins* and *Wartella, 1976; Wartella, 1979; Wartella* and *Alexander, 1978*).

A 40 % sample of all the late afternoon and evening TV series that involved family settings broadcast in Minneapolis-St. Paul, Minnesota area, during the 1975–76 season were taped for content analysis. These included three dramatic series – *Little House on the Prairie, The Waltons,* and *Swiss Family Robinson* – and six situation comedies – *The Brady Bunch, The Partridge Family, All in the Family, Good Times, Happy Days,* and *The Jeffersons.* For each series, we taped three shows during September, and two each during the following four months. Thus, eleven shows from each series were taped.

Behaviors portrayed on these programs were coded as being either pro-social or anti-social. Conceptually, pro-social behaviors are considered to represent a willingness to work with others in attaining goals, using socially acceptable methods. Anti-social behaviors, on the other hand, generally reflect an unwillingness to work with others, or the use of aggressive methods to attain goals. Robert *Liebert's* research provided the basis for the measurement of pro- and anti-social behaviors. In his research, five major categories of pro-social behavior and one category of anti-social behavior (aggression) are distinguished. In this study, the same main pro-social behavior categories were retained, but for each of the categories, anti-social behaviors at the opposite end of the same continuum were identified. The major categories of pro-social behaviors coded are altruism, expressing remorse, expressing concern for others, control of aggression, and resisting temptation. Major categories of anti-social behavior analyzed are: refusing altruism, refusing to express remorse, lack of concern for others, aggression and succumbing to temptation. There are many other social behaviors which are not clearly either pro- or anti-social such as conversational statements, joking, laughter and many nonverbal cues. These neutral behaviors, which in this research accounted for nearly two-thirds of the television characters' behavior, were not coded. About 150 behaviors were coded per half hour show, or one behavior every ten seconds. Coders viewed each show three times, stopping the show as often as necessary to fill in details regarding each behavior and verifying initial coding. Although coders had a relatively low agreement in their identification of behaviors to be coded (about 60 %), when there was agreement that a specific behavior was to be coded, there was high agreement on the behavioral category (86 %). Also, after all of the coding was completed, the coders always had high agreement on the total number of behaviors coded (within 10 %) and on the distribution of pro- and anti-social behaviors coded (mean correlation of .91 for the major behavior categories).

Several general comments about these family-oriented programs can be offered. First, we found these shows to be proportionately high in portraying pro-social behaviors. Across all shows, more pro-social behaviors were coded than anti-social behaviors. For instance, about half of all of the behaviors coded were in the pro-social category of showing concern for others in one way or another. One-seventh of the behaviors were expressive of altruism, sharing, cooperating and helping others. Anti-social behaviors accounted for one-fourth of all codable behavior. The major category of anti-social behaviors was instances of verbal aggression – yelling, shouting and insistent demands. A very low instance of physical aggression was found in these shows, which is understandable since these are family-oriented programs.

In addition to the strongly pro-social nature of these family-oriented programs, a second striking characteristic is the dominance of the father in the programs. Either the father dominated the show alone (*All in the Family, Jeffersons* and *Swiss Family Robinson*) or shared dominance with a child (*Little House on the Prairie*), or a child character dominated the programming (*Happy Days* and *Waltons*). In only three series, *Brady Bunch, Partridge Family* and *Good Times,* mothers shared dominance with one or more children. In no program series was the mother the *major* character in terms of behaviors portrayed; and this is even the case for a program like the *Partridge Family* which concerns a widow and her four children.

Not only do mothers not dominate these family-oriented programs, but they also present a relatively restricted range of behaviors: mothers are uniformly portrayed in pro-social terms, with 75 % of the 2,987 mother behaviors coded falling into the pro-social categories. Showing concern for others, followed by helping behaviors are two major types of pro-social behaviors expressed by mothers on television. What variation exists among the types of mothers portrayed on television is relatively minor. Consider the mothers on the four programs: *Little House on the Prairie, Partridge Family, Happy Days* and *All in the Family.*

78

Mrs. Ingalls of *Little House* and Mrs. Cunningham of *Happy Days* are very similar types of television mothers. Both shows have historical settings, *Little House* takes place in the Minnesota of the 19th century, while *Happy Days* portrays life in the 1950's. The mothers on both of these programs are overshadowed by their husbands and their children. Their major function in the program is to show concern for others – soothing their children and husbands or performing some sort of helping behaviors. Fully 85 % of the behaviors of Mrs. Cunningham and 90 % of the behaviors of Mrs. Ingalls fell into these two categories. Rarely do these mothers even express verbal anger: only eight instances of verbal aggression were coded of the 110 coded behaviors for Mrs. Cunningham, and nine instances of the 200 coded behaviors of Mrs. Ingalls were coded as verbal aggression. These women characters enact an extremely benign mother role; mother as caretaker, helper, and emotional support. That they are also dominated by their husbands and children is further indication of their relatively secondary role in the family.

Somewhat in contrast, but still highly pro-social are Edith Bunker of *All in the Family* and Shirley Partridge of the *Partridge Family*. Both Mrs. Bunker and Mrs. Partridge are contemporary women with adult children. Although Mrs. Partridge represents an upper middle class widow living in California and Edith Bunker portrays a working class housewife from New York, the two women share certain similarities of portrayals. These mothers are slightly more multidimensional than Mrs. Ingalls and Mrs. Cunningham. They are more visibly on screen than the earlier two mothers and elicited more codable behaviors. Furthermore, their behavior is more mixed. Only 55 % of the 363 coded behaviors of Edith Bunker represent showing concern for others while one-fourth of these actions represented rejection of affection and sympathy as well as selfishness. Furthermore, forty-six instances of aggressive behavior, primarily verbal aggression, was attributed to Edith Bunker. Shirley Partridge similarly expressed more mixed behaviors than other mothers studied: about half of her actions which were content-analyzed were found to be expressions of concern for others in the programs, however, she also was coded as expressing more aggressive behaviors than any other mother (29 % of the 252 coded behaviors fell into the aggression category). She was shown helping, sharing or cooperating 12 % of the time.

Thus, in these four mothers we have two strongly positive characters and two characters who although positive overall do exhibit somewhat more diversity in their behavior. None of these mothers, however, are less pro-social than any of the children or fathers portrayed on the family-oriented programs.

How do children perceive these television mothers? As part of a larger study of children's pro-social learning from television, we interviewed children regarding their impressions of television mothers. The data reported here were collected in the second wave of a panel survey conducted in October, 1975 and May, 1976 in St. Paul, Minnesota. The panel survey was designed to examine developmental changes in children's interpretations of television series and characters and the subjects' own social behavior. After ascertaining the frequency with which children viewed each of the nine "target" family-oriented programs the children were subsequently interviewed for their impressions of father, mother and child characters on each of two of these programs. Only the impressions of mother characters will be discussed here.

An open-ended question, similar to that used by *Lively* and *Bromley* (1973) was employed to measure children's impressions of the TV character. It asked the children to indicate the kind of person the character was: "Describe (character) so that someone would know what she was like and why she was like that." Interviewers recorded verbatim the children's responses to the task. Coding of the answers utilized a complicated coding scheme which indicated whether the child was making an interpretation in terms of appearance or identity characteristics, behavioral actions, or personality traits or motivations as well as whether the assertions about the character were positive (mention of pro-social characteristics), negative (mention of anti-social characteristics) or neutral. Subsequent to the impression description task the children were asked how much they liked the character and how realistic each character appeared to them.

In October, 1975, a random sample of 510 names of children were made from lists of students at five grade schools and two junior high schools in the Mounds View school district in suburban St. Paul, Minnesota. 420 children were interviewed in the Fall, 1975. The data reported here were collected in May, 1976 in follow-up interviews with 388 of the children, including 127 second graders, 138 fifth graders and 128 eighth graders. In each group, approximately equal numbers of boys and girls were interviewed.

The children were asked to give their impressions of mothers on shows of interest. Four television series dominated the interviews and therefore will be analyzed here: *Happy Days* was discussed by 244 children, the *Partridge Family* by 195 children and *Little House on the Prairie* and *All in the Family* were each discussed by 54 children.

Children's free descriptions of the characters were subsequently content analyzed into three major categories: identity/appearance characteristics, behaviors, and personality traits/motivations. Up to five assertions about each character were coded for analysis.

In general, children's free descriptions of television characters confirmed age-related findings of previous research on children's impressions of others. Children in the two youngest age groups, second and fifth grades, are more likely to describe characters in terms of appearance/identity characteristics or surface attributes than are eighth graders. Similarly, children in these two age groups are less likely than eighth graders to use trait/motivation assertions in their descriptions, although this relationship holds most strongly for the mother and child characters discussed. Fifth and eighth graders are more likely to describe characters in terms of behavioral actions than are children in the youngest age group.

Children's descriptions of the four target mothers, Mrs. Ingalls of *Little House on the Prairie,* Mrs. Cunningham of *Happy Days,* Edith Bunker of *All in the Family* and Shirley Partridge of *Partridge Family,* reflect the content analysis evidence. Overall, the children do perceive the mother character in strongly pro-social terms. Girls ($\bar{x} = 1.28$) are more likely to mention pro-social aspects of mothers when describing them than are boys ($\bar{x} = 1.09$). Very few neutral comments ($\bar{x} = .57$ for boys and $\bar{x} = .75$ for girls) and almost no anti-social references about mothers are made in these descriptions (boys $\bar{x} = .19$ and girls $\bar{x} = .10$).

In particular, Mrs. Ingalls of *Little House* is discussed in highly pro-social terms ($\bar{x} = 1.59$). The older eighth grade children are more likely to describe her as helping others (the main category of responses). Second and fifth grade girls mention more pro-social assertions than do boys. Male eighth graders mention an average of three pro-social assertions about Mrs. Ingalls in their description compared to 2.3 mentions for eighth grade girls.

Mrs. Cunningham of *Happy Days,* although strongly pro-social in the content analysis, is not perceived as positively by the children, particularly the boys. Girls at each grade level of second, fifth and eighth grades mention more pro-social comments about Mrs. Cunningham than do boys ($\bar{x}$ of pro-social comments by girls = 1.12 and by boys, $\bar{x} = .79$).

Shirley Partridge is viewed more positively by second grade girls ($\bar{x}$ frequency of pro-social assertions = 1.27) than boys ($\bar{x} = .63$), but similarly by fifth and eighth grade girls and boys. Edith Bunker again receives the fewest pro-social assertions (overall $\bar{x} = .78$) and the most anti-social assertions ($\bar{x} = .33$). This is the case for all grade levels and holds equally for boys and girls.

It would appear that the children's impressions of these characters' behavior fits fairly well their portrayals as content-analysed. The unidimensional Mrs. Ingalls is described in fairly unidimensional terms and the more mixed multidimensional Edith Bunker is similarly described in mixed terms.

Interestingly enough, there is little difference in the children's perceptions of the realism of these characters. The children were asked if these mothers act like mothers in real life. Answers were scored as yes, no and sometimes. Mrs. Ingalls, the most unidimensional mother, is perceived by the children in second and fifth grade as the most realistic mother (75 % of second graders and 63 % of fifth graders say she is like mothers in real life). In contrast, 70 % of eighth graders say she is sometimes like mothers in real life. Similarly, Shirley Partridge, a somewhat more mixed character is perceived as acting like a real mother by 60 % of the second graders, 65 % of the fifth graders and slightly more than two-fifths of the eighth graders. Approximately one-third of the children at each grade level perceives Mrs. Cunningham and Edith Bunker as realistic. There are no differences between boys and girls in their perceptions of the realism of these television mothers.

It would appear that these children perceive mothers in strongly pro-social terms and that this is realistic to them. The role of mother as nurturant and helper is perceived by children as appropriate to televised mothers. Mrs. Ingalls, the most strongly pro-social and unidimensional mother as discussed by the children, is also perceived as the most realistic mother.

One last question we queried the children about is their liking for the television character. Responses were obtained on a four point scale: not at all (1), not too much (2), a little (3) and a lot (4).

There was no evidence of age-related differences in children's liking of each of the television mothers discussed. Rather, there were strong differences between boys and girls. Girls by and large liked the mothers better than did the boy viewers, however, mothers overall are not well liked television characters. More females ($\bar{x} = 2.80$) like Mrs. Ingalls than do boys ($\bar{x} = 2.28$). This relationship also holds for Shirley Partridge (girls $\bar{x} = 2.75$ and boys $\bar{x} = 2.33$) and Mrs. Cunningham (girls $\bar{x} = 2.56$ and boys $\bar{x} = 2.29$). There is no difference in liking of Edith Bunker on *All in the Family* (girls $\bar{x} = 2.62$ and boys $\bar{x} = 2.68$). More striking than the sex differences in liking of television mothers though is the finding that mothers are uniformly *less* well liked than are television fathers or children (see *Wartella,* 1979).

Summary

Television mothers are strongly unidimensional people; they are pro-social characters, who tend to be overshadowed in importance by their husbands and/or children. In short, mothers are stereotyped as the soothing caretakers of their families. Child viewers apparently perceive these mothers in this manner, since all mothers were described by second, fifth and eighth grade children in strongly pro-social terms. The most pro-social mother discussed in this study, Mrs. Ingalls of *Little House on the Prairie,* is also the mother perceived as most realistic by the two younger age groups, second and fifth graders. More eighth graders (boys and girls) perceive Shirley Partridge (a slightly more multidimensional mother) as realistic than they do any other mother discussed.

Nevertheless, the children are not very fond of television mothers. Mothers on television are uniformly less well liked by all age groups than are television fathers or children. This is especially the case for boys, who dislike television mothers more than do girls. It may very well be that the relatively limited range of behaviors that mother characters enact, their lack of dominance in the series, and their relatively benign portrayals may lead the children to perceive them as less desirable people with which to identify.

Just as previous research has shown women on television to be generally depicted in narrow portrayals, it is clear that this restricted range of behavior also holds for television mothers. Television mothers are almost uniformly pro-social in depiction and they are perceived as such by child viewers. Neither are they very well liked as characters by these children. It would seem that greater diversity in portraying television mothers, showing them in a range of activities both outside and inside the home, might develop different expectations of the real life role of mother for these child viewers. There is little diversity in portrayals of mothers on television, and the children seem to accurately perceive this lack of diversity.

References

Lemon, J.: Dominant or dominated? Women on prime-time television. In: Tuchman, Gaye (ed.) et al.: Hearth and home. Images of women in the mass media. New York: Oxford University Press 1978.

Lively, W.J.; Bromley, D.B.: Person perception in childhood and adolescence. London et al.: Wiley 1973. XI, 320 p.

Sternglanz, Sarah H.; Serbin, Lisa A.: Sex role stereotyping in children's television. In: Developmental Psychology, 10/1974/5, pp. 710–715.

Tedesco, N.: Patterns in prime time. In: Journal of Communication, 24/1974/2, pp. 119–124.

Tuchman, Gaye (ed.); *Daniels, Arlene Kaplan* (ed.); *Benét, James* (ed.): Hearth and home. Images of women in the mass media. New York: Oxford University Press 1978. XI, 333 p.

United States, Commission on Civil Rights (ed.): Window dressing on the set. Women and minorities on television. A report. Washington, D.C.: U.S. Government Printing Office 1977. IX, 181 p.

United States, Commission on Civil Rights (ed.): Window dressing on the set. An update. Washington, D.C.: U.S. Government Printing Office 1979.

Wackman, D.; Collins, W.A.; Wartella, Ellen: Children's social learning from family-oriented television programs. Report to the John and Mary R. Markle Foundation. Minneapolis, Minn.: University of Minnesota 1976.

Wartella, Ellen: Children's impressions of television families. In: Dordick, H. (ed.): Proceedings of the Annual Conference on Telecommunications Policy. New York: Heath 1979.

Wartella, Ellen; Alexander, A.: Children's organization of impressions of television characters. Paper presented to the International Communication Association Convention, Chicago, April 1978. N.p.: n.pr. 1978.

Hertha Sturm, Marianne Grewe-Partsch

Time, television, and women's career perspectives*

This paper deals with the question of time perspectives as they relate to modes of presentation in television programming. It will be shown that these presentation modes have a bearing not only on perception but on how women tend to plan and conceive of their lives.

Our conception of time perspectives, it must be noted from the start, is continuously developing and is therefore subject to outside influences throughout our lives. We all know for instance that the thinking of a child is concerned with shorter time periods than that of an adult. For a young child a period of 14 days can be quite impossible to comprehend – though a grown-up has a clearly defined notion of a fortnight.

In addition, it is not only our awareness of time which gradually develops. The number of objects we can grasp and interact with, both mentally and physically, is also continuously increasing. The very young child fixes his or her attention first of all on one object – usually one he/she wishes to possess. A school-age child, however, is already in a position to cope with many objects at one time and to relate them to each other. He/she can play cards and chess according to the rules. With time, a young person is moreover able to move away from concrete references and to solve problems solely on the intellectual level. *Piaget* shows that with age we gradually free ourselves from simple stimulus/response reactions and develop an abstract formal logical way of thinking.

Thus, the multiplicity of our references to reality and our time perspectives are closely interlinked. The fewer the relationships we have learned to handle the more limited our perspective of time will be. Our capacity to deal with complex relationships and our capacity to master time are both learned through gradual processes – processes determined by outside stimuli. If a child, or human being for that matter, lives in total isolation, neither an awareness of time nor an understanding of the relationships between objects and concepts is developed. In fact, a human being living in total isolation, shut off from all outside stimuli,

---

* The paper was presented at the 27th Annual Conference of the International Communication Association, Berlin, June 1977.

simply dies. We may conclude, therefore, that the way in which our time perspective develops and the way in which we handle relationships, both complex and simple, depends on the environment in which we live and on the outside stimuli acting upon us.

Television is doubtlessly one of these outside stimuli. This raises the question: Do the typical presentation modes of television contribute to the development of a time perspective or do they, on the contrary, hinder such a development? Moreover, do the presentation patterns of television further or impede our capacity to handle a variety of relationships at once?

Answers must be found to these questions because they have a bearing on how people plan their future lives. This, after all, is the key problem we are concerned with when we talk about women and their personal and professional futures.

Unfortunately, virtually no work has been done on the effects of television presentation modes. Yet, this does not mean that indirect evidence is not available. Cumulatively, this evidence suggests what might be expected. Let us begin with the well-known popularity of advertising messages and commercials for children. A number of reasons have been given for this popularity by researchers but few of them have noted the fact that they are possibly preferred because they are short. Commercials do not demand attention for extended lengths of time. They consist of individual episodes and rarely contain the complete development of a story. Usually, the beginnings and ends of an action are conveyed in a matter of seconds. Also, single references and single points are conveyed with overemphasis rather than with differentiation. Consequently, the perception and understanding of commercials is a simple matter and there is hardly any risk of misunderstandings.

If we relate this simplicity and short duration to the perception structure of the preschool child, a number of points emerge. The younger the child the shorter his or her period of attention. Furthermore, the younger the child the greater the concentration on single points in the surroundings and the stronger the focus on individual, unconnected events. Textbooks on psychology note that the child's world is on a smaller scale than that of the adult. Not only the number of objects and events which can be assimilated at the same time is smaller, but the length of the child's attention focus is also shorter. Though the preschool child will always pick out certain partial happenings about the environment, actual life situations, in turn, offer opportunities for learning other kinds of selection patterns. This is not the case with commercials which have been pre-fabricated with a view to brevity, leaving little scope to improving and extending a child's selectivity.

All of these considerations raise a question of considerable importance about how perception patterns are learned. Psychological research indicates that perception patterns are not invariable. They change, instead, throughout a person's life. The child and the adolescent, in fact, gradually acquire and expand their capacities for dealing with stimuli and impressions coming from the environment.

How does television contribute to this development of capacities? As the normal child tends to steadily increase the complexity and time frame of his/her perception patterns, we must ask ourselves whether the prevalence of short television items does not encourage the adolescent to remain for longer than necessary at a perception level which he or she should have outgrown at an earlier age. The consequences of such a stunted development might be an inability to pay attention for longer time spans as well as an irritable boredom with situations where "nothing is happening".

Many current findings support this contention. Teachers note differences in the behavior of present-day school children compared with those of a generation ago. Although it is quite clear to us that subjective assessments are not conclusive, the frequent findings of lack of concentration, decreases in attention, and giving up when faced with difficulties, are phenomena noted for the first time in the generation of children and young people who have grown up with television. Even if we disregard this evidence, it becomes increasingly important to ask what is the nature of the influences of television which has become one of the important agents of socialization in our time.

To begin with, it can be assumed that anyone who watches television is always confronted with a multiplicity of subjects. In the case of programs using the magazine format a whole package of subjects is presented. Each of these in turn are presented in different formats. More importantly, however, the media-specific presentation modes of television foster and accelerate rapid change as compared to real life. There is no fixed camera angle comparable to that of the individual-centred visual angle of a particular observer. Instead, there are cuts, fades, changes in perspective, and montage. Continuity of picture and sound also do not exist and the viewer is confronted with jumps from picture to words and back again. In addition, person-to-person conversations with their pauses and redundancies do not exist; boredom and redundancy are eliminated. The viewer is required to absorb and reconstruct many short items day in day out. To do this a person must enter into a state of the "here and now" to cope with the constantly new impressions imposed by television. Although the viewer can neither control nor predict these impressions, reaction is inevitable. What he or she is confronted with is a media-specific stimulus/response barrage which is always of short duration. Would it not be reasonable to expect that such a state of affairs would leave perceptual traces?

In addition, it is well known that these presentation modes occur across topics and subject matters. It makes virtually no difference whether one is viewing a news presentation or a situation comedy. One must suspect consequently that presentation modes leave stronger impressions on the viewer than content. Such a prediction is backed by numerous findings which show that content has only limited impact on the recipient because of selective perception. It is well known that viewers generally select only those passages with which they agree. Those which are not to their liking are overlooked, overheard, or reinterpreted. The formal media-specific presentation modes of television, however, are likely not to be affected by selective perception because the viewer hardly notices them. Furthermore, programs themselves are not very stable. They are subject to group pressures and political influence which may remove them from the air at a moment's notice. The media-specific presentation modes in contrast are very stable and, what is more, very much alike. So even if a recipient is able to escape content which is unappealing – whether by program avoidance or through well-trained selective perception – television's media-specific presentation mode is ever present. Through constant repetition the viewer is gradually influenced and his or her views of the environment and cognitive assimilation processes will doubtlessly change.

In summary it should be noted that television provides and utilizes different kinds of short-term stimuli all at the same time. There is first of all the packaging of a variety of items especially in magazine type programs. Then there is the format of these items, *how* things are said, which are also short and capsulated. We are presented with opinions, results, news items in pictures as well as presentation modes of television which further accentuate the mosaic pattern of the medium through montage, cuts and "jumps" in picture and sound. All three of these factors require inclusion in future effects studies, but especially presentation modes require further attention.

A variety of studies concerned with short-term environmental stimuli can provide some clues about the ways in which presentation modes might affect the television viewer. Psychology, sociology and educational theory agree that the child and adolescent need to be freed from and grow out of the restrictive "here and now" framework in order to function effectively as an adult. Planning one's working career, partner relationships, and personal growth all require the development of long-term strategies and goals. One must learn to act in longer time and space sequences to consider and assess what has happened in the past and what the future holds. One must learn to defer wishes and needs so that these can be realized gradually.

One set of studies has noted that children from underprivileged families have particularly short attention spans and limited objectives. Such children consequently need things to be divided up into small pieces for logical simplification. Social scientists explain such "here and now behavior" as resulting from socioeconomic conditions. They note the short-term wage payments for workers and the inability of the worker to see how his or her work segment fits into the larger production process. Analyses of this kind give rise to such demands as increasing the training periods and the intervals between wage payments. Participation in decision-making is also recommended in order to demonstrate how present activity affects the future. The much discussed efforts for remedial action seem to be reducible to a common denominator. All of them call for the creation of a social environment in which a person can learn to deal with long-term objectives.

Such arguments and approaches seem to be strangely contradictory. There are on the one hand attempts to provide 20th century humans with strategies to increase their independence from the many short-term events which daily surround all of us. Adult education and counselling for careers, marriage, and family guidance are such strategies as are school advisory services, sales consultancies and advice on taxes and rent. Yet, at the same time the number of short-term happenings seems to be increasing in people's lives. Here one must mention the proliferation of leisure activities, replacability of children's short-lived technical toys, constant noise and telephone interruptions in cities, and the increased need for changes of scene of all kinds. In the light of this evidence and the psychological research previously noted television's reinforcing role of the short-term must be taken seriously.

What we have to ask ourselves in this context is how the medium of television works as a socialization factor. In what ways exactly does it contribute to both the short- and the long-term formation of viewers' sensibilities? The medium is capable of doing both, depending on the way its potentialities are actualized.

On the one hand, television provides many stimuli which contribute to the widening of horizons and incorporates stability through fixed program times and series which extend over weeks. Yet on the other hand, media-specific presentation modes do exactly the opposite. They foster a dependence on the "here and now" and demand that the viewer "joins in" in order to comprehend the myriad "jumps" in time, place and subject matter. Such a focus, it has been argued, hinders or even prevents the viewer from thinking actively about what he or she sees.

How should programmers and others deal with these contradictions especially with respect to young people's programs? One might ask oneself whether it would not benefit some children's programs to be paced a bit slower. Should there not be some scope for introducing the child's own ideas? Many of these are different from the way the programmers construct a given "here and now". Could not pauses be better arranged? And should not the line of a plot be presented in such a way that children can distinguish between main- and sub-plots, between what is important and what is "frills"? All of these questions indicate our concern that the preschool child in particular should not be cut off from further cognitive development as a result of television viewing.

Of course, it is possible to imagine a society of children and adults in which only quickly changing relationships count. A society in which something must perpetually happen to maintain people's simple-minded uncritical attention. The question is whether we want that kind of a society. And when it comes to the education of girls, should we not fight against these developments? Should we not instead try to liberate them from the all too limiting stimulus/response perspectives which are constrained by the "here and now"?

According to *Piaget* our capacity to develop different time perspectives on which our orientation toward the future is based varies with social class, with culture, and with sex. Girls grow up in an environment in which the short-term is much more prevalent than the long-term. Remember, for instance, that mothers are continuously performing short-term tasks such as washing dishes, making beds and cooking meals. These endeavours are furthermore interrupted by the demands of various family members. Several studies document that young women are more likely to take well-paid jobs immediately after high school rather than to embark on long-term studies providing the foundation for professional qualifications. One must ask oneself additionally how well these patterns fit with the apparent mutual exclusiveness which work and marriage choices seem to present for many women in our society.

Once again, it seems that television as a socializing agent may be particularly harmful to young women. As we argued earlier this medium socializes us as viewers to expect that a story's outcome will be presented within the next ten, twenty or forty minutes. In weekly magazine programs it encourages us to expect to be informed about the most complicated issues in less than five minutes. These expectations, deliberately aroused, are in complete contrast to life's realities. The intricacies of this reality cannot possibly be described using only simple, linear "if-then"-relationships. The same can be said about what young women are faced with when they are asked to define and conceptualize their futures in more than stereotypical terms.

It might be argued that our interpretation is just a thesis, that the evidence we have presented is no more than hypothetical, that it lacks empirical verification. To counter this assessment we want, in conclusion, to present some interesting and unexpected findings resulting from an experiment involving four to seven-year olds who were given the task to solve a Piaget-type problem with specially designed toys. A television film portrayed the freeing of a rabbit. To achieve this result, however, the children had to reenact, in game form, various tasks previously shown on the screen. They had to build a staircase, go through a tunnel, etc. The children achieved their goal and set the rabbit free. After this, however, surprisingly 80 % of them continued replaying the TV story in reversed order, although this had neither been demanded of them nor been shown on the screen. The end of the TV play, in other words, seems not to have corresponded to the children's internal time expectations.

This is clearly an example of the so-called "*Zeigarnik*-effect" well known to psychologists. The *Zeigarnik*-effect suggests that unfinished actions create tensions in the individual which are released only after an interrupted or unfinished task has been completed. The same effect is well known to all of us in the sense that it is unfinished actions which disconcert us, which keep on interfering with our thoughts, until we can at last complete them in one way or another. Think of the tax-form you have not yet filled out; of that letter you have failed to write; of the discussions you have put off; of the exams which remain untaken – the examples are endless.

In summary, it is important to note that psychological research confirms that the capacity to determine and strive for goals is related to a growing time perspective. It is related to the capacity to withstand frustrations, as well as to the ability to tolerate detours. All of this must be experienced and learned. A woman who experiences only short-term relationships will have difficulties in extricating herself from the here and now. Unfortunately, television – undoubtedly one of the important external stimuli in our lives – does not contribute to the development of a more extended time perspective. Yet, this does not mean that television is all bad. Surely, it also awakens interests and motivations. It raises interest in foreign languages, it encourages us to get to know foreign countries, it helps us to look forward to an interesting job and to free ourselves from the constraints of every-day life. But the question in relation to television, as we see it, is not merely how to motivate the viewer. It is rather how to make sure that life-enhancing motivations are strengthened so that the viewer may be equipped to deal more adequately with the myriad demands life places on each and every one of us daily.

References

Nickel, Horst: Entwicklungspsychologie des Kindes- und Jugendalters. Ein Lehrbuch für Studierende der Psychologie, Erziehungs- und Sozialwissenschaften. Bd. 2: Schulkind und Jugendlicher. 2nd rev. ed. Bern et al.: Huber 1976. 531 p.

Piaget, Jean: Psychologie der Intelligenz. 5th ed. in the completely revised translation of the 2nd ed. Olten et al.: Walter 1972. 196 p.

Salomon, Gavriel: Sesame Street in Israel. Its instructional and psychological effects on children. N.p.: n.pr. 1974. VII, 105 p., 19 p. appendix.

Singer, Jerome L.; Singer, Dorothy G.: Can TV stimulate imaginative play? In: Journal of Communication, 26/1976/–, pp. 74–80.

Sturm, Hertha: Fernsehen und die Entwicklung der Intelligenz. In: Ronneberger, Franz (ed.): Sozialisation durch Massenkommunikation. Stuttgart: Enke 1971. pp. 290–304.

Sturm, Hertha: The application of Piaget's criteria to television programmes for children. In: Werner, Peter (ed.): Information programmes for children 7–12 years old. Geneva: European Broadcasting Union 1977. pp. 12–19.

Sturm, Hertha: Die kurzzeitigen Angebotsmuster des Fernsehens. In: Fernsehen und Bildung, 9/1975/1, pp. 39–50.

Sturm, Hertha: Medienwirkungsforschung – ein Faß ohne Boden? Oder: Plädoyer für eine konstruktive Alternative. In: Fernsehen und Bildung, 10/1976/3, pp. 161–168.

Sturm, Hertha: Fernsehdramaturgie und Zeigarnik-Effekt. In: Fernsehen und Bildung, 11/1977/1-2, pp. 103–110.

Sturm, Hertha: Emotionale Wirkungen. Das Medienspezifische von Hörfunk und Fernsehen. Ergebnisse aus zwei Untersuchungen und Weiterführungen. In: Fernsehen und Bildung, 12/1978/3, pp. 158–168.

Zeigarnik, Bluma: Das Behalten erledigter und unerledigter Handlungen. In: Psychologische Forschung, 9/1927/–, pp. 1–85.

Gertrude Joch Robinson

Changing Canadian and US magazine portrayals of women and work:
Growing opportunities for choice

In every society, sex-gender associations are the most pervasive aspect of so-cialization. They associate values and attributes with feminine and masculine behavior which are particularly inflexible in North American and European Ju-deo-Christian societies. In these societies the private realm is the woman's and the public realm is the man's, which means with respect to employment that work outside the house is negatively evaluated. Women's life planning conse-quently is fraught with contradictions. It must try to harmonize notions of "proper" with prestigeous career choices, "fulfilling" work with marriage and childbearing. For many women these choices are mutually exclusive and there-fore difficult to make. Adequate career training and preparation are conse-quently often neglected ultimately preventing women from developing auton-omous roles outside the home.

Within living memory these public roles have however been socially and legally sanctioned in both North America and Western Europe. World War I gave fe-males the vote and the second war legitimized middle class married women's participation in the labor force for the "national good". As a result of these and other lifestyle changes (*Ridley,* 1968)[1] by 1976 over half of all U.S. and Canadian women between 18 and 64 were working. In addition, most of these women were married and had pre-school children. In the last decade as a matter of fact, working mothers with children under six were the fastest growing segment of the work force in a North American economy increasingly requiring informa-tion processing rather than production skills (*Tuchman,* 1978).[2] Such a trans-formation affects not only women themselves, but their families and their co-workers. In the light of these massive social changes the media portrayal of women's working lives becomes a topic of great social concern. Have the media kept up with women's new public roles or are their portrayals still dominated by traditional values left over from an earlier age?

Two complementary types of answers have been offered as to why the media are important. The first notes that the media select, structure and evaluate what

93

is considered important and good in the public discussion agenda (*Shaw* and *McCombs*, 1977).[3] All media and especially television which seems to be the only institution creating messages for *all* of us, help in the public definition and legitimation of life and work in a variety of ways. They grant notice of the existence of certain kinds of work activities. They also specify, contrast and describe the work behavior of different groups of people and they bestow approval or censure on this behavior. Public recognition, description, and legitimation are essential for women who wish to challenge and upgrade their public right to work (*Gusfield*, 1966).[4]

In addition, the media serve as "reference groups" for audience members. "Reference groups" are groups with which a person compares him- or herself in making a self-judgment. Mass media portrayals thus are important because they help define the appropriateness of certain kinds of jobs for women, the satisfactions women may expect from work outside the home and how it should fit in with their traditional family responsibilities. All of these in turn influence the choosing, planning and execution of careers for those young women who will be filling available jobs in the 1990s.

Media portrayal of women and work: Alice in her Wonderland

A variety of writers have noted that the media are selective and that they tend to reflect the dominant and socially accepted values. Two major theories explain this media selectivity. They are based on divergent assumptions about the nature of media functioning and social reality. The more prevalent one supported by network personnel and advertisers asserts that social reality is fixed and that the media simply "objectively" and passively "reflect" certain aspects of this reality. The media in this view are like fun house mirrors, providing a somewhat distorted picture of what is "out there". The other position asserts, following *Burke* and *Cassirer,* that social reality is actively created and recreated through the different meanings people attach to it (*Burke*, 1963).[5] Media portrayal in this view is a "construction" process in which what is selected is not random. It is instead the product of bureaucratic practices which stress organizational needs more than personal outlooks (*Robinson*, 1978).[6] Media content, consequently does not reflect a looking-glass likeness, but takes on an "Alice in Wonderland" distortion full of unmapped "black holes" which obliterate issues and attitudes which do not fit in with prevailing values and norms.

94

This paper adopts the second position and explores both the constructions and the unmapped "black holes" in the portrayal of women's lives in order to explain why they are what they are. In line with the "construction" theory it inquires more specifically into three questions: (1) whether there are differences in different media portrayals of working women; (2) whether there is a difference between pre- and post-1970s portrayals, and (3) whether there is a difference between Canadian and U.S. renditions and outlooks.

A variety of studies have noted that television, the most ubiquitous medium, is also the one most likely to "ignore" women through lack of coverage in its news presentations or trivialization in advertising and situation comedies (*Tuchman,* 1978).[7] The reason given is that this medium programs for a large heterogeneous audience, not particularly concerned with women's lives. In contrast, newspapers with their women's sections, or women's magazines sponsored by advertisers wishing to attract a female audience, should be more responsive to changing attitudes toward work. Furthermore, socio-linguists like *Labov* have noted that there is a time lag in the appearance of changing private values in public discourse (*Labov*).[8] For the portrayal of women's changing work activities, this might mean that there is less evidence of women's changing public roles before 1970 than after. We would expect to find more emphasis on women's home roles during the 1940s through 1960s than after the rise of the women's movement and its support for women's careers, egalitarian pay and freer lifestyles. Finally, it is worth finding out whether the emerging portrayals of women's roles is similar in North American and Western European societies where women's participation in the public realm was differentially supported depending on whether the vote was granted in the 1920s or later (*Black,* 1978).[9]

To test these three hypotheses concerning the portrayal of women in their home and work roles, two types of research were undertaken. The first scrutinized short stories in women's magazines and updates earlier studies investigating the life and work characteristics of magazine heroines in the pre-1970s period. The second is broader and more ambitious. It maps for the first time whether and how women's changing lifestyles are being portrayed in non-fiction articles. This pilot study investigates the prevalence of and preferred themes related to women in and outside the home between 1970 and 1977. In doing so we will be able to determine whether this coverage is broader than that offered by television and to discover possible differences in themes and emphases in Canada and the United States where women (except in Quebec) received the vote early.

Magazine images of women and work before 1970: The "happy housewife heroine"

To get at the pre-1970s data, the existing American research literature was scanned and evaluated. This evaluation revealed that little has been written on the magazine portrayal of women's lives. As few as seventeen articles cover this topic broadly defined. Nearly one-third of these (six articles) concentrate on the characteristics of magazine heroines.[10] Another third (five articles) investigate social norms, sex roles and passivity in working class romance and middle class magazines.[11] Two deal with women's magazines in general and their growth and change.[12] Three investigate children's awareness of occupational differences between the sexes as well as occupational advice and problems of working women.[13]

Out of this collection we decided to focus on the life characteristics of magazine heroines in order to determine implicit attitudes towards work. Betty *Friedan*, the first to analyze short story heroines, discovered that women with careers declined drastically in the twenty year period between 1939 and 1959. In 1959 most of the heroines of *Ladie's Home Journal, McCall's, Good Housekeeping* and *Woman's Home Companion* were career women. Ten years later only one in three of the heroines had a career and by 1959 only one woman in a hundred even had a job. The happy housewife heroine was clearly dominant (*Friedan,* 1963).[14]

Bailey's update of 1957 and 1967 heroines in the same publications adds that the anti-work trend continued and that heroines were getting younger. In the ten years there was a further decrease of characters with careers from 9 % to 4 %. Career women who did appear, were moreover never sympathetically portrayed. They were usually pictured as "unwomanly" and were seen most often in the act of threatening some "true" woman's marriage (*Bailey,* 1969).[15]

Another study by *Franzwa* of the same magazines adds detail on the extent of sex-stereotyping found in the heroines' jobs. Following generally accepted notions of "proper" work for women, most magazine heroines were employed in low status jobs, if they worked at all. 51 % were employed as secretaries, clerks or in service positions. 38 % were in medium rank positions such as nursing, primary school teaching, flight attendant or writer. An infinitesimal 7 % had professions entailing long preparation like college professor, geologist or museum director. A few characters earned a substantial income as interior decorators or owners of businesses (*Franzwa,* 1974).[16] This researcher reiterated that about two-thirds of all female characters were married and that of the married women in the stories only a small 11 % held jobs outside the house.

My own study, designed to further elucidate the relationship between marital status and work in the same U.S. plus two Canadian magazines (*Chatelaine* French and English versions) further corroborates and extends the *Franzwa* findings.[17] In the 1968 to 1970 period the typical magazine heroine was white middle class (91 %), under 35 years of age (78 %), married (58 %) and living in marital bliss (71 %). Only 33 % of all characters were single, divorced or widowed, with the remaining 8 % having an unspecified status. For most heroines (58 %) the level of education was not indicated, whereas the educational achievements of males were generally noted. Most of the married women were housewives (73 %) with only 15 % working outside the home. Generally the heroines had no stated goals in life (52 %) though if a goal was mentioned, it was love-oriented (27 %). Only 2 % of the heroines had career goals.

In all of the stories the possibility of dual roles was implicitly rejected by the mere fact that only 15 % of the heroines were both homemakers and worked. Furthermore, dual-role lives were generally portrayed as "fragmented". Consequently, even in the 1970s these heroines tended still to give up their job in favor of full-time home-making and motherhood. In case this route was not chosen, the heroine is portrayed as the evil career woman, inhuman and unwomanly, defying the "laws of nature" (*Robinson,* 1971).[18] To top it all off, only one out of 125 married characters feels discontented with her housewife role, but this "delusion" lasts only as long as her 24-hour flu. Seventeen years after *Friedan's Feminine Mystique* none of the heroines had as yet recognized "the problem that has no name".

Conclusions: To work is "unwomanly"

In spite of changing social mores, magazine fiction up to 1970 reflects a strong bias in favor of the homemaking role for woman. It extolls the "passive" female as the ideal, irrespective of class and culture. Such passivity reflects itself according to *Flora* in ineffectuality, non-initiative in problem solving, non-participation in the labor force and lack of social mobility (*Flora,* 1971).[19] Magazine fiction furthermore defines women in terms of men and families rather than in terms of work. As such it tends to denigrate married working women which by now constitute a sizable minority of the 1970's work force. In the United States 41 % of the female labor force were married in 1970 and six years later in Canada the figure is even higher, 54 % (*Waite,* 1976).[20]

The fiction furthermore reiterates that work does and should play a secondary role in women's lives. This runs counter to the fact that women with husbands in the lowest and mean brackets must seek employment to supplement inadequate family incomes (*Connelly,* 1976).[21] In addition, working mothers are placed in a double bind. They are portrayed as causing the disintegration of their family's life if they persist in working. Yet, eroding family incomes and increased consumer goods orientations indicate that women's salaries are vital to maintaining a North American middle class life style in the 1960s (*Bell,* 1976).[22]

The negative evaluation of work extends even to single magazine heroines, only about half of which work. The rest of these women study (8 %), engage in leisure activities (15 %), are home-makers (4 %), or have this area of their lives unspecified in the fiction (14 %) (*Robinson,* 1971).[23] The cumulative impact of such a description of women's lives is not only highly selective and out of tune with reality, but negative and discouraging in terms of the example it sets. It fails to provide alternative outlooks for women readers struggling to gain insight into the changing nature of their surroundings.

The portrayal of women's changing lifestyles in the 1970s

To begin to understand whether women's roles in and outside of the home are more broadly covered since the rise of the women's movement, the second and more ambitious pilot project gathered data of a different sort. Interviews with magazine editors such as Doris *Anderson* of *Chatelaine* indicate that magazine fiction is perhaps not the best index of a magazine's attitude and understanding of women's lives, because it is produced by freelancers over whom the editor has little control. *Anderson* herself longs "for the day when the consciousness raising exercises in the analytic and scholarly books are translated into fiction." Yet as editor she cannot do more than encourage her freelancers to incorporate modern trends into their stories (*Anderson,* 1971).[24]

Our study was therefore designed to systematically map post-1970 non-fiction articles in three types of magazines to assess what kind of an interpretation of women's roles they offer. Three different kinds of magazines, women's, elite and general news, were selected because one of our initial hypotheses suggested that women's magazines may be most responsive to women's changing lifestyles.

In order not to have to sample total magazine content, it was decided to focus on a few themes which are judged relevant and indicative of modern outlooks.

Such an analysis however hinges on a distinction between traditional and nontraditional content which is difficult to make. Only one author, *Guenin's* study of changing women's sections in daily newspapers attempts such a definition (*Guenin,* 1975).[25] Based on interviews with modern lifestyles editors, it isolates 24 topics of potential interest to modern women. Our study utilized 8 of these to begin mapping modern trends and "blind spots" in magazine interpretations of women's public lives in the 1970s. *Guenin* categories adopted are: work, women's movement, feminism, equal rights, marriage and divorce, single life, population control and education. In addition three more categories were suggested by our own research: women in politics, history, and art.

Table 1 indicates that the nine magazines in the three types were chosen for their large circulation, their prestige as determined by age and Canadian or U.S. representation. The general magazines are: *Time, Reader's Digest* and *Maclean's* (Canadian). The elite magazines are *Atlantic Monthly* and *Saturday Night* (Canadian), and the women's magazines include: *Good Housekeeping, Ladies' Home Journal, McCall's,* and *Chatelaine* (English version). These magazines constitute not only the leaders in their field, but were also the sources for the magazine heroine studies mentioned above. Some comparability between the findings of the pre- and post-1970s is thus provided.

Table 1: U.S. and Canadian magazines and their circulations

Categories	Magazine names	Circulation 1977	Original publication year	Yearly issues
General News:				
	Time	4,2 mi.	1923	52
	Reader's Digest	17,7 mi.	1922	52
	Maclean's (Canadian)	6,7 mi.	1895	12
Elite:				
	Atlantic Monthly	325,000	1857	12
	Saturday Night (Canadian)	100,000	1887	12
Women's:				
	Good Housekeeping	6,0 mi.	1895	12
	Ladie's Home Journal	7,0 mi.	1882	12
	McCall's	6,5 mi.	1870	12
	Chatelaine (Canadian)	1,0 mi. (Engl.) 275,000 (French)	1919	12

Source: National Research Bureau, Working Press of the Nation, Vol. II Magazine and Editorial Directory, Chicago, 1978 pp. VII, 1-82.

Our nine magazines in the pilot study are of course not a representative sample, since there are upward of 980 consumer magazine titles listed in the 1978 Working Press of the Nation's *Magazine and Editorial Directory*.[26] They do however provide a first approximation for indicating potentially different patterns of coverage in the three magazine groups. They also provide evidence for differences in national approaches. According to the *Magazine and Editorial Directory,* general magazines are the largest category with 120 titles. Women's magazines are second with 63 publications, and news magazines are one of the smaller sub-categories with 30 entries. All together the three contain 213 titles, approximately one quarter of all listings. In our pilot study the year, title, topic, sex of author, length and placement, as well as the evaluative dimension (writer's attitude toward the topic) were scored for each article. These provide data for an assessment of the impact of a writer's sex on coverage as well as for yearly fluctuations. All in all a total of 1316 issues were scanned and 948 articles analyzed.

Work, marriage and feminism capture primary attention

To begin to understand what is "newsworthy" and interesting about women's lives in the 1970s, Table 2 provides data on the most heavily covered topics in the three magazine groups. Leaving out content concerned with such traditional themes as children, health, home, food, and beauty, it appears that there are four high scoring areas of coverage. In order of priority these are: women and their work situation: 261 stories; marriage and divorce: 205 stories; issues of feminism: 126 stories, and women's activities in politics including 81 stories. Though these categories are generally self-explanatory, it is important to note that the topic of "feminism" subsumes articles on consciousness raising, women's changing awareness in relation to the outside world as well as the issue of rape. The "women's movement" topic in contrast includes only articles dealing with *organized* women's groups, their progress, issues, conventions, and relationships.

Table 2 shows additionally that general news magazines also feature women and work in first place, though they place feminism second, and marriage and divorce third. Elite magazines in contrast have as their most covered topic "woman in art"; doubtlessly as a result of the fact that these magazines are published for an urban elite in the art centers of New York and Toronto. The topics of work and feminism however follow in second and third place, as in the other two magazine groups. Women's movement stories are in fourth place.

Table 2: Magazine topics by magazine type 1970–1977 (Nos. of Stories)

Topics	General Magazines				Women's Magazines				Elite Magazines		Totals	
	Time	Digest	Maclean's	McCall's	Good House-keeping	Ladies' Home Journal	Chatelaine	Atlantic Monthly	Saturday Night		Nos.	%
Women and work	45	25	38	30	18	65	26	10	4		261	(28)
Women's movement	21	4	2	0	3	–	3	7	1		41	(4)
Feminism	32	15	29	26	4	4	15	–	1		126	(13)
Marriage and divorce	12	58	4	22	13	70	18	7	1		205	(22)
Equal rights	13	5	4	1	2	4	4	6	4		43	
Population control	11	5	–	3	–	–	7	–	–		26	
Single life	1	25	3	4	6	3	2	4	1		49	(20)
Education	3	7	–	1	–	1	9	2	–		23	
Abortion	14	5	2	4	2	–	5	1	1		34	
Day care	1	3	–	1	1	1	6	–	–		13	
Politics	4	–	16	17	7	14	8	3	3		81	(9)
History	–	2	–	–	2	4	–	4	3		15	(1)
Art	–	–	11	3	1	–	–	10	6		31	(3)
Rape	–	–	–	–	–	–	–	–	–		–	
Sub Total	157	163	109	112	59	166	103	54	25		948	(100)
Group	429				440				79			

101

When total number of articles are converted into percentages, Table 3 indicates that the public discussion agendas of the three magazine types are surprisingly similar, an outcome which had not been expected. They all cover the same topics though in slightly different orders of priority. Such a finding suggests that it is both premature and difficult to argue that women's magazines are more responsive to women's needs *in general* than general news or elite magazines. The only point that can be made is that women's magazines concentrate the most *total* attention on the four topics and that they are most concerned with the problems of working women. An overwhelming 71 % of all women's magazine articles are devoted to work, movement news, feminism, marriage and divorce. General news and elite magazines on the other hand concentrate only 66 % and 51 % of all articles respectively on these topics. In addition, women's magazines do the most work coverage, nearly a third of the total (31 %) of their articles are devoted to such stories. General news magazines have one quarter and elite magazines less than a fifth (18 %) work articles.

Table 3 offers the additional insight that general news and elite magazines provide more *variegated* coverage of women's affairs than the women's magazines which are still heavily pre-occupied with the issues of marriage and divorce (28 %). The topics of equal rights, single life and sexual equality, abortion and population control garner better coverage in the magazines written for a mixed female/male audience.

Table 3: Magazine topics by magazine type 1970–1977 (in %)

Topics	General News Magazines	Women's Magazines	Elite Magazines
1. Women and work	25	31	18
2. Women's movement	6	1	10
3. Feminism	18	11	10
4. Marriage and divorce	17 (66)	28 (71)	13 (51)
5. Equal rights	5	3	1
6. Population control	4	3	0
7. Single life	7	3	6
8. Education	2	3	3
9. Abortion	5	2	3
10. Day care	1 (24)	2 (16)	0 (13)
11. Politics	6	10	7
12. History	1	1	9
13. Art	3 (10)	2 (13)	20 (36)
	100	100	100

The similarity of topics selected in all three magazine groups suggests that audiences are possibly less important in determining content than the professional judgements of staffs. Such an interpretation would fit in with substantial evidence that producers try to protect their "monopolies of knowledge" from outside influence and criticism. This is achieved by the fact that producing staffs form elites which know each other and furthermore share the same work techniques (*Tuchman*, 1966).[27] They also structure audience surveys in such a way that these polls query only preferences among *available* rather than *possible* content categories. All of these factors encourage similar topic selection among different magazine types produced for different audiences.

Global figures however provide only a first approximation for evaluating the question of quality. May it be that women's magazines are more detailed and variegated in their portrayal of women's work problems than the general news and elite publications written for a mixed audience? To unravel this issue the following section will provide a more detailed content analysis of the "women and work" articles.

Women and work: The struggle for job equality

Previous tables show that "women and work" had the highest total number of articles, 261 out of 948 and that this topic was most heavily covered by the women's magazines. Considering the many possible ways of covering such a topic, it is however extremely interesting to note that Table 4 confirms that *all* articles of whichever magazine type have only two major foci: 46 % of all stories cover the struggle for job equality, and 24 % of all articles concentrate on work discrimination. A staggering 70 % of all interest is thus placed on such issues as: equal pay for equal work and improved access to male jobs as well as discrimination at the work place. Three additional topics: dual role problems, first women, and profiles constitute the remaining topics of discussion. Such a finding does not permit us to conclude that women's magazines provide a broader and more sensitive portrayal of women's work problems.

Selected titles of job equality articles indicate that women's entry into sex segregated positions, a broadening of career possibilities, and a concern with career planning are the primary issues discussed in *all* three magazine groups. "She thinks like a man: Women move in business," *(Saturday Night)*; "Women in the boards" *(Time)* about the lack of corporate representation of women; "Police woman on patrol," *(Reader's Digest)*; "Which professions pay off for women," *(Chatelaine)*; "Return of the mid-wife" *(Good Housekeeping)* and "Guerilla

Table 4: Numbers of "women and work" articles by theme in three magazine types

Magazine type	Job discrimination	Job equality	Family and work	First woman	Profile	Row total
Elite:						
Atlantic Monthly	3	2	2	0	1	8
Saturday Night	1	3	1	0	1	6
Sub total	4 (28%)	5 (37%)	3 (21%)	0	2 (14%)	14
General News:						
Time	15	22	0	1	5	43
Reader's Digest	3	15	5	0	4	27
Maclean's	2	14	3	0	19	38
Sub total	20 (19%)	51 (47%)	8 (7%)	1 (1%)	28 (26%)	108
Women's:						
Ladies' Home Journal	28	23	5	4	8	68
Mc Call's	2	23	4	1	0	30
Good Housekeeping	1	3	4	0	7	15
Catelaine	7	14	3	0	2	26
Sub total	38 (28%)	63 (45%)	16 (12%)	5 (3%)	17 (12%)	139
Grand total	62 (24%)	119 (46%)	27 (10%)	6 (2%)	47 (18%)	261

guide for working women" *(McCall's)* give an inkling of the coverage. Job discrimination situations and their remedies are recounted in "All those thinkies, all those thoughts" *(Atlantic)* about women in academia; "The hand that rocks the cradle rules the newsroom" *(Maclean's)*; "Father make her a priest" *(Time)*; "How the trade unions let women down," *(Chatelaine)* and "You can fight sex discrimination on the job" *(Good Housekeeping)*.

Profiles with 18 % of all articles constitute the third focus of "women and work" stories. This is a relatively safe category permitting editors to talk about "first women" in a particular post or recounting an exceptional woman's entry into public, artistic and political life. Cynically viewed, such reporting is a form of tokenism, satisfying the need to show that women are moving out of the home and are "making it" in the world that counts. The relative dearth of "first women" stories, which are very prevalent in daily newspaper reporting, however provides cause for rejoicing. It indicates that magazine editors at least feel that by now women have penetrated into virtually every job category and that this penetration in itself is far less important than the kind of treatment females encounter in the work world.

The most interesting and potentially explosive topic "family and work" however garners only a miniscule 10 % of all article attention. Why do so few articles refer to dual role stress which affects more than half of all working women? Interestingly enough the articles do not even reflect this fact, but talk primarily about the plight of single women or heads of households juggling both jobs and children. One might speculate that the potential implications of work equality for family life are entirely too revolutionary to contemplate. A careful treatment including the equalization of housework and childcare would raise questions about the implications of the paternalistic family system which even socialist countries have not been willing to face *(Scott,* 1974).[28]

In analyzing "women and work" articles we were additionally interested in determining whether magazine type, sex of author, readership, and article length are systematically related to positive evaluation. Table 5 tracing these interconnections indicates that in women's and elite magazines, where the majority of articles are written by women, positive evaluations are as frequent as in general news magazines, many of which do not indicate authorship. Length furthermore is associated with type of magazine rather than with topic. General news magazines carry overwhelmingly (77 %) short articles of less than 75 square inches. Women's magazines had 52 % medium articles of 76–150 square inches and elite magazines had 79 % of their articles in the large, over 150 square

Table 5: Author's sex, evaluation and location of "women and work" articles in three magazine types

Magazine Category		Author's Sex			Evaluation			Length			Type of Article		
		F	M	Not listed	+	–	0	lg	med	sht	ed.	feat.	gen. art.
General News	No	37	28	43	76	10	22	15	10	83	0	37	71
	% (108)	34%	26%	40%	72%	8%	20%	14%	9%	77%		34%	66%
Women's	No	109	10	20	78	5	56	34	71	34	12	52	75
	% (139)	78%	7%	15%	56%	4%	40%	24%	52%	24%	9%	37%	54%
Elite	No	8	6	0	11	1	2	11	2	1	2	4	8
	% (14)	57%	43%		79%	7%	14%	79%	14%	7%	14%	28%	58%

inch category. Since all of the readers in our nine magazines are middle class and no investigation of editorial attitudes was made, it is impossible to tell whether these factors are positively associated with pro-coverage or not. These findings correspond closely to those of *Farley,* who found that there were no correlations between author's sex, length of article, and positive evaluation. In her analysis of equal rights legislation coverage in women's magazines, positive correlations did however emerge between editorial policy, large circulation, and middle class readership (*Farley,* 1978).[29]

Conclusions: Cautious optimism

How does our evidence fit in with other researchers' findings on the portrayal of women's lives in the 1970s? One study summarizing recent investigations paints a very grim picture. It speaks of the "symbolic annihilation" of women in television, about women's magazines carrying the message "marry and don't work," and about newspapers retaining the notion that women are important only as consorts to famous men (*Tuchman,* 1978).[30] *Corea* rounds out this dismal picture by adding six additional as well as depressing criteria, which explain women's newsworthiness in the press. They are: beauty, victimization, political significance, performance in the arts or athletics, special home-maker abilities, and first woman status (*Corea,* 1973).[31]

As we noted elsewhere, such newsvalues tend to make women-related items rarer, shorter, and lower in the line-up of typical television newscasts.[32] They also encourage the selection of female newsmakers of lower status, e.g. without organizational affiliation, and portray their activities as less important. Women in broadcasting this study confirms are disproportionately associated with human interest events, disasters or women's activities, all of which are not rated "top of the news" (*Robinson, 1978*).[33]

While symbolic annihilation and victimization are certainly the lot of women in television portrayals, our comparative magazine data suggest a more optimistic picture. Magazines in contrast to the broadcast media seem to be more responsive to the major issues facing women in the 1970s. Contrary to expectations, this includes not only women's, but all three magazine types.

Comparing the pre-1970s heroine studies with post-1970s non-fiction coverage, our evidence shows that the dictum "marry and don't work" has in fact been modified. Popular concern is today focused on women and work, changing marriage and divorce, as well as issues of feminism and the womens' movement. Such an ordering of the public discussion agenda suggests more than a "quiet concern" for women's changing roles. What we are witnessing is the widespread acceptance of certain egalitarian tenets of the women's movement reflecting the desires of both men and women to provide equal opportunity for choice of life style. Among these are everyone's right to work if they wish, a concern with making marriages more congruent with both partners' needs, the desirability of encouraging women to re-think their own roles, and the acceptance of those feminist values stressing self-knowledge and development which will ultimately ensure a better life for all.

The substantial coverage accorded women in politics, history, and art suggests furthermore that certain public roles are not only well established, but approved for women as well as for men. Studies of news coverage suggest that this acceptance is a result of their being a part of the traditional beat structure in daily press and television news gathering, which have historically legitimated male politicians, artists, and historical figures (*Robinson, 1978*).[34] Women as latecomers are beginning to reap the social prestige associated with these institutionalized media roles.

The remarkable shift to greater acceptance of women's search for new roles outside the home, including greater work participation, our evidence suggests, is however linked with a concomitant reluctance to investigate how this equalization of work and other opportunities is to be *practically* achieved. Our identification of minor themes in Table 2 indicates that there are six themes which together receive only 20 % of total coverage in all magazine groups. These minor themes give us clues as to the "blind spots" in magazine coverage. They refer to the areas of equal rights legislation, population control, single life, educational equality, abortion, and day care.

In the same vein our more detailed analysis of work articles indicates that our society is not yet ready and willing to publicly explore the practical implications of dual roles on marriage and children. We are not yet clear about the rules according to which nurturing roles will be divided in the future. On what basis and by whom career and work sacrifices are going to be made and how paternity and maternity leaves are going to be arranged.

Our survey of "blind spots" thus suggests that what is being covered in all magazine types are those themes with which we feel more comfortable, and for which there is greater public consensus. Topics which raise real challenges about the restructuring of the patriarchal family set-up are generally left out. As *Huber* notes "Lenin and the early feminists were optimistic about the contributions of technology in liberating women. Yet, 'technological change' resulted in men's monopolizing the exchange of valued goods and services, while women monopolized increasingly trivialized domestic work and second class jobs owing to their childbearing responsibilities." (*Huber,* 1975)[35]

Cautious optimism that the "symbolic annihilation" of women at least in the magazine field is slowly coming to an end is finally found in a series of articles assessing the impact of the women's movement today (*Tuchman,* 1978).[36] Out of eight, only two articles entitled "Requiem for the women's movement" (*Harper's,* 1977) and "Beyond sisterhood" (*Weekend Magazine,* 1977) come to the conclusion that the women's movement "has narrowed to a pallid lobby for equal rights." Using such tactics as discrediting, isolating, and undercutting, which are tactics still successful in television, these articles attempt to ridicule the legitimate claims of an out-group which constitutes 51 % of the total population (*Gerbner,* 1978).[37]

The majority of articles however paint a more serious and careful picture. They draw attention to the legal, work, political, and social changes which have resulted from the movement and comment that it has become an integral part of most people's lives. The headlines note: "The women's movement is alive and kicking" (*Chatelaine,* 1977), "Lib lives" (*Homemaker's Magazine,* 1977), "Ten years of women's liberation" (*Weekend Magazine,* 1978), "Moving on and reaping the rewards of the women's movement" (*New York Times Magazine*, 1978) and "Building the feminist network" (*Saturday Night*, 1978).

Bonnie *Kreps* summarizes their message in "Lib lives" and indicates how coverage has broadened since 1970, when the topic first received public notice (*Robinson*, 1978).[38] In 1977 it is possible to evaluate the women's movement in the following sympathetic way: "For the first time in history, as far as we can tell, we have a movement with no overall structure, with no membership cards, with no leaders, with no one, agreed upon political platform, with no hierarchy. That is the great strength and beauty of this movement. It is a movement intended to bring about a transformation in our most basic human values and as such it cannot be evaluated in the usual way, on the basis of quick success in gaining a power base, or in terms of the tired and stale rhetoric of our competing political parties. It is to the change in the very fabric of women's lives that we must look for success, and any public fight that can be seen as leading toward that goal is worth fighting" (*Kreps*, 1977).[39]

Cautious optimism, finally, is warranted with respect to the narrowing gap between material conditions and changing attitudes toward women's entry into public life and work. More and more evidence is now available that younger generation women have a more liberal value outlook toward sex roles than their mothers. In 1977, a New York Times CBS news poll found that fully three-quarters of those aged 18 to 29 preferred the idea of shared marriage roles and believed that women should work. In the 45 to 64 age bracket only 41 % and 48 % respectively were of these opinions. *Ingelhart* believes that these differences are permanent results of socialization patterns of generations of people growing up in particular environments (*Ingelhart*, 1971).[40]

Black's comparison of US and Canadian attitudes on women's participation in public life found similar generational differences in outlook. Once again generational attitudes towards the statement that "politics should be left to men" show women and men aged 65 and over in partial agreement with the statement while those in their thirties, twenties and teens disagree strongly. The figures for women are 50 %, 65 %, 72 % and 78 % disagreement while the comparative figures for men are: 52 %, 63 %, 68 % and 67 % (*Black*, 1977).[41] *Black* concludes that "it is the young women of this generation who have encouraged the breaking down of the barriers between private and public, making sexuality a political matter with their demand for an end to legal restrictions on contraception and abortion, making childcare a public obligation with their demand that it be provided for all parents. In generational terms, the "acquisitive" women of the post suffrage period staked out women's claim to access to men's public realms. But it is post-bourgeois women who are opening up the private realm to men and thus to all of us. Men should be sympathetic to this endeavor.[42]

Such similarities in North American outlook suggests that U.S.-Canadian differences in the portrayal of women's lives is probably minimal, because both countries adopted women's suffrage about the same time. Support of women's legal right to enter the public arena has existed for over fifty years in both countries. Table 6 which compares *Maclean's, Chatelaine,* and *Saturday Night* themes with U.S. averages in the three types of magazines confirms this hunch. Canadian magazines cover the same themes in the same order as their counterparts south of the border. 5 % to 10 % differences exist however in "women's movement" and "marriage/divorce" coverage and in feminism, politics, and art. Whether these fluctuations from the average are significant is however not determinable from our small sample.

Two types of conclusions for future comparative research emerge from these findings. The first notes that "generation" must be added to "sex" as an additional and crucial predictor of magazine content. All of our magazine groups, irrespective of whether they were edited for female or mixed audiences, defined women's changing roles in the same manner, because they have to attract more

Table 6: Canadian-US comparison of magazine topics (in %)

Topics	Gen. News Mags.		Women's Mags.		Elite Mags.	
	Maclean's	U.S. aver.	Chatelaine	U.S. aver.	Sat. Night	U.S. aver.
Women/work	35	25	26	31	16	18
Women's movement	2	6	3	1	4	10
Feminism	26	18	15	11	4	10
Marriage/divorce	4	17	17	28	4	13
Minor Categories						
Women in politics	15	6	8	10	12	7
Women in history	0	1	0	1	12	9
Women in art	10	3	0	2	24	20

Based on data in Tables 2 and 3.

readers from the younger/middle than the older, after 55 year generations. The second conclusion suggests that nationality differences too are perhaps tempered by inter-generational similarities. The reason for this is that both the North American and the Western European countries gave women the vote about sixty years ago and thus laid the foundation for the public legitimation of changing female roles. Young men and women alike have internalized these more egalitarian value outlooks and are beginning to apply them to the private and the public realms on both sides of the Atlantic.

Footnotes and References

[1] *Ridley, Jeanne Claire:* Demographic change and the role and status of women. In: Annals of the American Academy of Political and Social Science, 375/1968/1, pp. 15–25.

[2] *Tuchman, Gaye:* The symbolic annihilation of women by the mass media. In: Tuchman, Gaye (ed.) et al.: Hearth and home. Images of women in the mass media. New York: Oxford Univ. Press 1978. p. 4.

[3] *Shaw, Donald L.; McCombs, Maxwell E.:* The emergence of American political issues. The agenda-setting function of the press. St. Paul: West Publishing Co. 1977. X, 211 p.

[4] *Gusfield, Joseph:* Symbolic crusade, status politics and the American temperance movement. Urbana, Ill.: Univ. of Illinois Press 1966. pp. 1–15.

[5] *Burke, Kenneth:* The grammar of motives. Los Altos: Hermes Publications 1963.

[6] *Robinson, Gertrude Joch; Sparkes, Vernone:* International news in the Canadian and American press. A comparative news flow study. In: Gazette, 22/1976/4, pp. 203–218.

[7] *Tuchman, Gaye,* op. cit., p. 7.

[8] *Labov, William:* On the mechanism of linguistic change. In: Giglioli, Pier (ed.): Language and social context. Harmondsworth: Penguin Editions, 1970.

[9] *Black, Naomi:* Changing European and North American attitudes towards women in public life. In: Journal of European Integration, 1/1978/2, p. 227.

[10] The six articles are: *Friedan, Betty:* The feminine mystique. New York: Del Publishing Co. 1963. pp. 26–63. *Bayley, Margaret:* The women's magazine short story heroine in 1957 and 1967. In: Journalism Quarterly, 46/1969/2, pp. 364–367. *Robinson, Gertrude Joch* (coll.); *Gardiner, Christine* (coll.); *Kirmayer, Wendy* (coll.) et al.: The image of women in American and Canadian magazines. Montreal, Québec: McGill Univ. 1971. *Johns-Heine, P.; Gerth, H.:* Values in mass periodical fiction, 1921–1941. In: Public Opinion Quarterly, 13/1959/1, pp. 105–113. *Franzwa, He-*

len: Working women in fact and fiction. In: Journal of Communication, 24/1974/2, pp. 104–109. *Phillips, Barbara E.:* Magazine heroines. Is MS just another member of family circle? In: Tuchman, Gaye (ed.) et al.: Hearth and home. Images of women in the mass media. New York: Oxford Univ. Press 1978. pp. 116–130.

11 The five articles are: *Flora, Cornelia Butler:* The passive female. Her comparative image by class and culture in women's magazine fiction. In: Journal of Marriage and the Family, 23/1971/8, pp. 435–444. *Gecas, Victor:* Motives and aggressive acts in popular fiction. Sex and class differences. In: American Journal of Sociology, 77/1972/4, pp. 680–696. *Smith, Dwayne; Matre, Marc:* Social norms and sex roles in romance and adventure magazines. In: Journalism Quarterly, 52/1975/3, pp. 309–315. *McCallum, Pamela:* World without conflict. Magazines for working class women. In: The Canadian Forum, –/1975/55 654, pp. 42–44. *Haymes, Howard:* Post-war writing and the literature of the women's liberation movement. In: Psychiatry, 38/1975/11, pp. 328–332.

12 The two sources are: *White, Cynthia L.:* Women's magazines 1893–1968. London: Joseph 1970. 348 p. *Ferguson, Marjorie:* Women's magazines. The changing mood. In: New Society, 29/1974/3, pp. 475–477.

13 The three articles are: *Clarke, P.; Esposito, V.:* A study of occupational advice for women in magazines. In: Journalism Quarterly, 43/1966/3, pp. 477–485. *Boef, Ann:* Doctor, lawyer, household drudge. In: Journal of Communication, 24/1974/2, pp. 142–145. *Hatch, Marya G.; Hatch, David L.:* Problems of married and working women as presented by three popular working women's magazines. In: Social Forces, 37/1958/1, pp. 148–153.

14 *Friedan, Betty,* op. cit., pp. 30–37.

15 *Bailey, Margaret,* op. cit., p. 366.

16 *Franzwa, Helen,* op. cit., p. 106.

17 All of these studies were based on a sampling of *McCall's, Ladies' Home Journal* and *Good Housekeeping* short and short short stories with a well-defined female character. Novels and novelettes were excluded because they were often not written specifically for women's magazines. Content categories include: marital status, appearance, economic class, education, major occupation, number of children, residence, housing, quality of marriage, goals and problems on which story is based.

18 *Robinson, Gertrude Joch* et al., op. cit., pp. 3–6.

19 *Flora, Cornelia Butler,* op. cit., p. 540.

20 *Waite, Linde:* Working wives 1940–1960. In: American Sociological Review, 41/1976/2, p. 65.

21 *Connelly, Patricia M.:* The economic context of women's labor force participation in Canada. Halifax: St. Mary's Univ. 1976. p. 4.

22 *Bell, Carolyn Shaw:* Working wives and family income. In: Chapman, Jane R. (ed.): Economic independence of women. New York: Sage 1976.

23 *Robinson, Gertrude Joch,* 1971 op. cit., p. 5.

24 *Anderson, Doris:* Real women in fiction where are you? In: Chatelaine, 14/1971/9, p. 1.

25 *Guenin, Zena Beth:* Women's pages in American newspapers. Missing out on contemporary content. In: Journalism Quarterly, 52/1975/1, pp. 66–69, 75.

26 Working press of the nation. In: Magazine and editorial directory, vol. 2. Chicago: National Research Bureau, Directory Division 1978.

27 *Tuchman, Gaye:* Objectivity as strategic ritual. In: American Journal of Sociology, 77/1972/1, pp. 660–670.

28 *Scott, Hilda:* Does socialism liberate women? In: Experiences from Eastern Europe. Boston: Beacon Press 1974. Chapter 3.

29 *Farley, Jennie:* Women's magazines and the ERA. Friend or foe. In: Journal of Communication, 28/1978/1, pp. 188, 190.

30 *Tuchman, Gaye,* op. cit., pp. 3–4.

31 *Corea, Gena:* Writer says papers biased in covering news of women. In: Editor and Publisher, 106/1973/April 21, p. 62.

32 A woman-related item is one which either has a female newsmaker, a female reporter or falls into women's content as defined by Guenin.

33 *Robinson, Gertrude Joch:* Women, media access and social control. In: Epstein, Laurily Keir (ed.): Women and the news. New York: Hasting House 1978. pp. 93–97.

34 Ibid., pp. 89–90.

35 *Huber, Joan:* Toward a socio-technological theory of the women's movement. Urbana, Ill.: Univ. of Illinois 1975. p. 1.

36 *Tuchman, Gaye:* The newspaper as a social movement's resource. In: Tuchman, Gaye (ed.) et al.: Hearth and home. Images of women in the mass media. New York: Oxford Univ. Press 1978 pp. 186–217.

37 *Gerbner, George:* The dynamics of cultural resistance. In: Tuchman, Gaye (ed.) et al.: Hearth and home. Images of women in the mass media. New York: Oxford Univ. Press. 1978. pp. 46–50.

38 *Robinson, Gertrude Joch:* Women, media access and social control. In: Epstein, Laurily Keir (ed.): Women and the news. New York: Hasting House 1978. pp. 97–103.

39 *Kreps, Bonnie:* Lib lives. In: Homemakers magazine, –/1977/Sept., p. 112.

40 *Inglehart, R.:* Changing value priorities and European integration. In: Journal of Common Market Studies, –/1971/Sept.

41 *Black, Naomi,* op. cit., p. 238

42 Ibid., pp. 237–238.

Mariann Jelinek

Career management and women*

Introduction

In October, 1969, Elizabeth *Janeway* began a review by noting,

> Half the human race is female. It is sometimes difficult to remember this, even for a female: and never more difficult than when reading history. Until late yesterday afternoon (speaking in terms of historical time) women intruded so rarely on the course of events that their total omission would hardly be noticeable.

We might adopt these comments almost without change, if we substitute the words "management studies" or "professional career studies" for "history", with no loss in meaning. The reasons are not far to seek. In management, as in history, our focus has traditionally been on those who lead, decide, strategize, use power. Typically, this has meant men. It still does. The overwhelming majority of large business firms in the United States are still managed by men – even today, some 15 years after the passage of Equal Economic Opportunity legislation, some six or seven years after the onset of lawsuits pressuring for change. Of 3.2 million people listed in the 1970 census as "managers and administrators" earning $10,000 or more a year, only 4,8 % were women. A *Fortune* magazine study on 1,220 major corporations and 6,500 top executives earning above $30,000 yielded only 11 women.[1] Most women are primarily concentrated in entry-level, supervisory, or trainee positions. The *Wall Street Journal* estimates that women hold only 6 % of all middle-management posts, and only 1 % of positions at vice presidential or higher levels.[2] By another popular measure of success, salary, professional women also fall far behind their male colleagues: only some 1 % of working women make over $10,000 per year, in comparison with 13 % of working men. A female college graduate is more likely to be underemployed, and may well earn less than a male high school graduate.[3] A recent survey of members of the Academy of Management, mirroring findings for other academic disciplines, noted that female respondents lagged their male counterparts of the same age substantially in salary.[4]

---

* The paper was presented at the 27th Annual Conference of the International Communication Association, Berlin, June 1977.

114

A shift in focus

But while women have not yet captured the bastions of power in the academic business community, or in the business community at large, changes are occurring. There are more women in managerial positions, even if at entry level; there are more women on corporate boards of directors; and there are many more female applicants for professional degrees including the MBA (Master of Business Administration). The *New York Times*[5] says that women presently constitute about a third of law school graduates, and an increasing proportion of top-flight business school graduates. According to a recent survey, in 1975–76, some 207 women appeared on 237 corporate boards: 80 of these appointments were made in 1975.[6] *Business Week* estimated 400 women on corporate boards in 1976, and described them as "exceptionally able people" who made their professional mark when women had to be outstanding merely to survive.[7] Women used to be appointed to boards to represent "the woman's point of view". That day is passing – today's women directors may protest that role. Not long ago, most would have felt obliged to champion women's causes without question. Now, it is permissible to disagree, to examine the assumptions, or to pay attention to other things entirely.

A similar broadening of perspective is visible in writing on women. The first generation of "women's studies" was political and polemical. Authors sought to prove discrimination and assert women's rights. Consciousness raising had a place, especially when a major aspect of the problem was the seeming invisibility of women as managers in the business world or as research topics. But it also had costs: polemic and consciousness raising polarize positions and impede free communication by arousing feelings of threat.

At least one sociologist, Nathan *Glazer,*[8] claims that our entire approach to affirmative action is dysfunctional, because EEO records-keeping requirements in essence treat people as group members – women, blacks, Spanish surname – rather than as individuals. The consequences, he claims, are a growing divisiveness and increasingly discriminatory attitudes as we get used to thinking of one another as group representatives. While *Glazer* focuses on blacks in his books, many similar questions might be raised about EEO as it applies to women. A major problem – both for women and for minority group members – is that at present there is little rigorous empirical work to base conclusions on: we just don't know. And we won't, until we have more sophisticated research that tests some of these assumptions, and more sophisticated models that have conceptual room for alternative explanations.

Perhaps the strongest inference to be drawn from an examination of research on women and careers is of the need for a thorough re-thinking of most of our concepts and theories and paradigms – about women, about careers, about work and its meaning for adults. This means going well past polemic.

The need for new models

More recent studies are far more sophisticated. The conceptual models employed are vastly expanded in that they no longer seek to prove discrimination, but rather to explicate observed differences by unearthing the underlying mechanisms. The shift is of the utmost importance. As a recent study on "Women and the Academic Labor Market"[9] noted,

> To summarize the direct discrimination discussion, what is often argued as per se evidence of discrimination can be interpreted as reflecting differences in life-cycle accumulation of professional skills. To resolve this question, it would be necessary to examine the earnings patterns of women who do work full time throughout their careers and should therefore have comparable levels of acquired skill.

This study concluded that "the potential role of direct discrimination against women is much smaller than is suggested by the wage differential unadjusted for detailed work history" (p. 213). In contrast, Mary Townsend *Hamilton*[10] concluded that wage discrimination does have a sex dimension, and that the estimated sex differentials generally exceeded those related to color, often by considerable amounts. Her study concerned non-professional white- and blue-collar workers.

Still another recent study focuses directly on management. Margaret *Hennig* and Anne *Jardim*[11] reported on an on-going study that has so far surveyed some 3000 women and 1000 men who have responded to a questionnaire assessing attitudes, expectations, career plans, experiences, and backgrounds. *Hennig* and *Jardim* conclude that women do indeed differ from men – and that a major source of difference has been dysfunctional attitudes and expectations held by women about their work, their careers, and their colleagues. They offer constructive advice for women seeking successful management careers. The conceptual framework on which the research is based is quite apparently *not* "let's prove discrimination", but rather "let's explore attitudes, backgrounds, and expectations for the light they might cast upon differences in careers". Like *Johnson* and *Stafford,* and *Hamilton, Hennig* and *Jardim* seek to go beyond the notion of "discrimination" as a single, monolithic explanation of differences between male and female career experiences. In so doing, they employ a conceptual framework not bounded by polemic bias. Such frameworks include the means of testing for alternative, less obvious, and far more useful explanations than "discrimination". In the process, all these studies pose critical questions of the assumptions that all differentials are due to deliberate discrimination that can be legislated out of existence, and the stereotypic assumptions about the experience of women that purport to explain all differences. These studies go well past polemic in shaping more inclusive, muscular models. They are, I believe, indicative of a new direction in research on women.

Attitudes and change: Emerging similarities

A similar shift in the attitudes of women in management roles seems also in evidence. Just as writing on women has moved well past the defensive stance of seeking to explain all differences as "discrimination", many women in management positions now treat "discrimination" as one of a series of problems they face as managers – of no overriding emotional importance, merely one facet of reality to be dealt with. A study by *Litterer*[12] notes that, while all members of his "successful women manager" category reported encountering sex discrimination upon entering managerial work, "all looked at the matter as a problem that could be solved or at least handled satisfactorily for their purposes". In contrast, women in a larger sample who did not meet criteria for the "successful" sample held another view:

> For some of these, problems so embitter their lives that this seriously interferes with their professional, and often personal lives. Others took up the cause of righting this injustice and made it the paramount focus of their careers. Still others became so dispirited that they came to doubt their own competency, [and] they either just stagnated in one position, or quit.

An on-going study of graduates of the Harvard Business School by *Harlan* and *Jelinek*[13] found similar evidence. Most women mentioned discrimination, but the majority saw it as one problem among many in establishing a successful career – not the only problem, or even the most important. One woman in their sample recounted her relief at finding that her consulting colleagues held stereotypic views of her career expectations: "It was simple ignorance on their part, not malice; they honestly didn't realize that I might be interested in a promotion to a job requiring substantial travel!" Still others told of strategies – ranging from "super-competence" to direct confrontation over beers to humor to persistence – which they used to overcome discrimination when encountered.

Some fascinating differences between women and men did emerge in the *Harlan-Jelinek* study: To a much larger degree, women tended to be the children of highly educated parents. Their mothers typically worked, most often in business or education: 40 % of the women reported mothers who worked, while only 29 % of the men did in a subsample matched for age, year of graduation, and job experience prior to HBS (Harvard Business School). Some 21 % of the women reported that their mothers held graduate degrees (31 % that their mothers had at least "some graduate or professional school"). In contrast, only 6 % of the men reported mothers' graduate degrees (13 % of the mothers had "some" graduate education). All this suggests that strong maternal role models are quite important for the women who choose to undertake an MBA at Harvard – with its reputation for challenge, pressure, overload, and its monetary and advancement value. Clearly, for these women, both parents tended to provide reinforcement and emphasis on *serious* education, and on education as an appropriate arena for competition and accomplishment for their daughters.

Another fascinating difference concerns marriage. While 60 % of the subsample women are married, 81 % of the men are married. Of those women who are married, many have no children, although they frequently comment that they plan children "eventually". Members of the sample tend to marry after HBS (somewhat later, for the women, than national norms). Spouse's occupation highlights another difference between the men and women: men are most frequently married to housewives, who may have a college degree but rarely more. The women are typically married to men who are professionals or businessmen with graduate degrees; as one might expect, many of the women are married to HBS graduates. The women appear to value education highly in choice of mates.

A more arresting trend visible in the *Harlan-Jelinek* data concerns changes taking place over time, rather than sex-related differences. Substantial numbers of respondents in the *Harlan* and *Jelinek* study, both male and female, reported concerns with "career direction" or "career progress". These concerns highlight an underlying similarity far greater than apparent differences. Other similarities emerge as well. The early "occupational segregation" of women in "women's jobs" is beginning to break down – for female graduates of the Harvard Business School at least. More women report direct managerial line responsibility – in manufacturing, for instance. One route to the top – through line responsibility – has traditionally been more direct.[14] For both sexes, job-related problems centered on learning to do the job, and on coping with interpersonal difficulties (although women more frequently described the problem as "getting through the system"). Amidst these similarities one substantial change does stand out over time (ranging from the class of 1962 to the class of 1975): there was an increasing concern with "non-traditional" issues. For both sexes, balancing the demands of a professional career against personal needs and family life was a major concern. The most apparent conclusion to be drawn from these data is that older respondents are more alike than different, regardless of sex; and younger respondents are more alike, regardless of sex. The younger males are more like the younger females than either group is like their older same-sex predecessors. In a subsample split by year of graduation (half the sample graduating before 1969, half after), older graduates typically seemed to have a more stereotypic separation of responsibilities toward home and children (where there were children), with women spending more time than men. However, the younger sample spent typically more time with family than the older sample – regardless of sex. Of course, this might partially be explained by the age of children, for younger children require more attention. But *both* parents in this sample seem to be spending more time. Here again, the younger graduates are more alike, regardless of sex, than either sex is like its same-sex predecessors.

Women as a group seem less successful than the men: they rank below their male colleagues on salary (82 % of the women in the sample had salaries of less than $ 3000 per month in the total sample, while only 51 % of the men fell into this category). As to level of hierarchy, 69 % of the men were at upper to top levels of management, while only 37 % of the total sample women were. The differences are larger for the older graduates than for the younger, as might be expected in light of continuing recent pressure towards greater equality on the job.

Toward more complex models

These findings highlight a critical problem for women and minority group members, and for the social sciences taken as a group. Though stereotypes abound, providing "explanations", there is at present relatively little empirical work relating to women and minority group members in management upon which to base conclusions – much of what has been done to date has failed to transcend the biases of current cultural stereotypes. We won't have answers to key questions about the possibly differing experiences of men and women, or whites and others, until we have more sophisticated research – with conceptual frameworks that have room for similarities as well as differences, and explanations more complex than simple "discrimination". The difficulty is that a great many of our theories, concepts and paradigms – about people and their work, about careers and career patterns and choices, about the meaning of work for adults – are drawn from research on male, middle-class, white Americans.[15] Just as most executives, even today, are white, male and middle-class, so most existing research on management has been based on this sample. Consequently most of our present theory is based on limited data. Utilizing these concepts for women and minority group members is, at best problematical – especially as a growing body of research suggests that attitudes may be more distinctive across an age or experience spectrum than across sex. This is true even for such seemingly sex-free concepts as identity, self-esteem, involvement in work, vocational maturity, occupational choice, and career path. Although *Blau* et al.[16] noted as long ago as 1956 that occupational or career choice was not made once and for all at adolescence, the obsolete model is still with us, only beginning to fade after 20 years. Women's work experience is a factor in its demise.

Many women – if not most – have multiple careers, as workers, wives, and mothers. If the choice was *either* career *or* family, it is most frequently now a choice of timing. Most women work; and most working women are married, with husband present. The sheer increase in female participation in the workforce has motivated a search for better models that can explain women's experience as well as men's. A number of stereotypes are falling in the process. Thus, in 1928 *Hogg* might assert that women work for convenience, as a "stopgap" before marriage – when, presumably, they left the workforce for good. If women ever typically married and left work permanently, however, that does not presently seem to be the case. In 1974, some 35 million women worked, constituting 45 % of all women over 16 years of age and over, and 39 % of the labor force as a whole.[17] Even the woman who does marry and stay home to raise children will typically find herself re-entering the labor force at about 40, with some 25 years of work-life ahead of her. Unless our paradigms have conceptual space for women as serious, long-term members of the workforce, our models are incomplete. Unless our models of career choice are complex enough to encompass multiple sequential or simultaneous involvements – like parenthood *and* professional life – they are insufficient. And not only on account of women. A study by the US Labor Department, based on 1970 census data, noted that nearly one in three American workers gave up their jobs and "changed careers" in the five-year period 1965–1970.[18] *Fortune*[19] corroborated the *Harlan-Jelinek* survey finding that personal life was increasingly important to men as well as women. In accounting for his company's corporate headquarters move away from New York, General Telephone and Electronics chairman Leslie H. Warner cited the increasing primacy of managers' personal lives:

> A much more important reason for the move was the growing difficulty we were having getting bright young people in our subsidiaries to accept promotions that required them to transfer to our headquarters in Manhattan. In some cases we offered to double their salaries, in one case from $30,000 to $60,000, but we still got turned down. The money, the promotion – it wasn't enough to lure them.
>
> Mind you, I admire these young executives for refusing transfers because they think it would hurt their private lives. We never did that in my day. I wish we had.

This sounds much more like the stereotypic expectations of women in the workforce – although *Litterer's* sample of successful women would all move and work things out with their husbands, if a move was required. In short, our stereotypes may well be misleading, and our concepts of career involvement and identity must include substantial room for variances – variety may be more the rule than the older stereotypes.

The experience of women at work hitherto has been demonstrably different from that of men. This different experience, besides demanding expanded conceptual models, may indeed generate alternative insights applicable to the work experience of males as well. Women typically have multiple careers, as workers, wives, and mothers. Each of these careers imposes substantial demands which may well conflict with the demands of another role. Of the women in the *Harlan-Jelinek* study, 60 % were married, and typically reported spending 20 hours a week on household and family tasks. Few men reported so heavy an involvement in home activities, yet a growing body of evidence suggests a long-term trend toward equality in parenting demands and household responsibilities, particularly in the growing number of dual-career families.[20] Some investigations of women's role conflicts and coping strategies in dealing with the multiple demanding roles of wife, mother, and worker; little research exists on the impact of this type of conflict for men. These trends suggest that more research is needed.

Research on women's role conflicts has given new prominence to the non-work aspects of adult life, and to multiple or sequential career patterns. Attention to women's careers has coincided with increased interest in developing all human potential. As a result, career options are expanding for both women and men, with increasing divergence from the old model of irrevocable, linear career choice. Whether or not a man decides to become a "househusband", staying home to take care of children and household as his primary career, his choices and involvement with family and non-work facets have both been significantly expanded. The female pattern of sequential careers (work following time out for childbearing) is mirrored in the "retread" phenomenon, where people go back to school, perhaps for substantial training, or undertake a very different second career after lengthy involvement in a first. It had always been done, of course; but now it's perhaps more common. Certainly much more attention is being paid to the whole idea now.

Besides expanded career options, investigations of women's experience suggest how people cope with conflicting demands. This kind of research would seem particularly fruitful for managers, whose overload situation is endemic. Women who successfully manage their multiple roles may well provide some hypotheses to be tested in the world of managerial work. *Hall*[21] identified structural role redefinition, in which the demands of the situation are restructured, as by negotiation with a superior, as the most effective strategy employed by women to cope with role conflict. The structural role redefinition strategy identified by *Hall* involves a proactive, self-defining approach. This is an apt description of the response of the G.T.E. executives, cited earlier, who redefine their response to exclude automatic acceptance of promotions that entail heavy personal costs. A priori, such a response would seem to offer the greatest likelihood of resolving conflicting role demands, as well as the greatest amount of personal autonomy. Both would appear to be powerful motivators for the entrepreneurial, enterprising, initiating personality types most frequently identified among managers.

The woman manager's situation suggests some other directions for research and some other gaps in our understanding. EEO demands substantial numbers of female and minority group managers, and also building new responses into our organizations in response to changed policy directives. *Murray*[22] notes that there was no discernible difference in the public statements and official policies of those companies who *did* implement EEO directives from those who *did not*. However, in those that did not, lower-level managers were convinced that what the top wanted was really the same old thing. Clearly, this suggests an abundant need for research in institutionalizing change, no less than a need for more data on the factors that do make for a successful career path. We need to know a good deal more about identifying, training, and nurturing successful managers. And here, too, the changing trend in research on women may offer some insights. The shift in focus, from proving discrimination to investigation of causes underlying observed differences, has lead to increasing attention to success factors. But research here is only beginning; much remains to be done. The outcome of such research will undoubtedly be much better management of managers at all levels, both male and female, better use of the scarcest resource of competent human beings.

Conclusions

Research on women at work, and particularly on women as managers, is at once in its infancy and in transition. The time for polemic is past, and new conceptual models are being forged. More research and more information are needed to flesh out these models. In particular, we need:

1. More investigations of role-conflict in men;
2. More thoughtful considerations of "non-traditional" career patterns – which well may be more common than uncommon;
3. Continued careful re-examination of our stereotypes and assumptions in explaining adult career paths.

The implications are far-reaching, and by no means limited to women. Many of our paradigms and concepts about work, management, leadership and a host of other managerial topics are drawn from limited samples, chiefly of male, middle-class, white Americans. And many of the norms and expectations we bring to research were shaped in drastically different social situations from those we face today. Thus a great many of our tools for investigation – those same paradigms and concepts – must be re-thought and recast to include the very different experiences of women, the very different attitudes and expectations of a great many managers – male and female – that seem to be emerging. Perhaps the largest single factor to be taken into account is the increasing participation of women in the workforce, as managers, and as wielders of power. Drastic shifts in the number of women directors mentioned here are only a small corner of the picture.

The re-thinking of so many concepts is difficult especially because the underlying task is to frame new models that question the very assumptions upon which our present concepts rest. We need all the openness we can derive from the less defensive, less contentious approach to women's research, to get past the seductively attractive conclusions suggested by polemic. And we need all the creative theory building we can bring to bear, to enrich our range of possible explanations. If our re-thinking is well done, we will more easily bring social policy into reality.

Footnotes and References

[1] *Janeway, Elizabeth:* The subordinate sex. An essay review of William L. O'Neill's 'Everyone was brave. The rise and fall of feminism in America'. In: The Saturday Review, –/1969/Oct. 11.

[2] Wall Street Journal, –/1977/April 26.

[3] *United States, Dept. of Labor, Women's Bureau* (ed.): Underutilization of women workers. Washington, D.C.: Women's Bureau, Workplace Standards Administration 1972. p. 17. "The educational backgrounds of a great many women are not being fully utilized in their jobs. A startling 7 per cent of employed women who had completed 5 or more years of college were working as service workers (including private household), operatives, sales workers, or clerical workers in March of 1969. Nearly one-fifth of employed women with 4 years of college were working in these occupations, as were some two-thirds of those who had completed 1 to 3 years of college."

[4] *Stead, Bette; Mullins, Terry Wayne:* The professional status of male and female Academy of Management members. Paper to be presented at the 37th Annual National Meeting of the Academy of Management, 1977. N.p.: n.pr. 1977.

[5] New York Times, –/1977/May 1, Business and Finance.

[6] Who are the women in the board rooms? In: Business and Society Review, –/1975-1976/16. Thirty-three of these women are noted as having a family affiliation with their companies.

[7] Business Week, –/1977/January 10.

[8] *Glazer, Nathan:* Affirmative discrimination. Ethnic inequality and public policy. New York: Basic Books 1976. 248 p.

[9] *Johnson, George E.; Stafford, Frank P.:* Women and the academic labor market. In: Lloyd, Cynthia B. (ed.): Sex, discrimination, and the division of labor. New York: Columbia Univ. Press 1975.

[10] *Hamilton, Mary Townsend:* Sex and income inequality among the employed. In: Annals of the American Academy of Political and Social Sciences, 405–410/1973/–, pp. 42–52.

[11] *Hennig, Margaret; Jardim, Anne:* The managerial woman. Garden City, N.Y.: Anchor Press Doubleday 1977. XVII, 211 p. See also: Psychology Today, –/1977/Jan., and: The New York Times (Business and Finance Section), –/1977/May 1, p. 4.

[12] *Litterer, Joseph A.:* Life changes of successful women managers. Paper presented at the 1976 National Meeting of the Academy of Management, Kansas City, Mo.: N.p.: n.pr. 1976.

[13] *Harlan, Anne; Jelinek, Mariann:* Career development project. Work in progress. Data from interview transcripts, field notes and preliminary data analysis.

[14] *Schein, Edar H.:* The individual, the organization, and the career. A conceptual scheme. In: Journal of Applied Behavioral Science, 7/1971/–, pp. 401–426.

[15] *Osipow, Samuel H.:* The relevance of theories of career development applied to special groups. Problems, needed data, and implications. In: Picou, S. (ed.) et al.: The career behavior of special groups. Columbus, Ohio: Merrill 1975.

[16] *Blau, Peter M.* (coll.); *Gustad, John W.* (coll.); *Jesson, Richard* (coll.) et al.: Occupational choices. A conceptual framework. In: Industrial and Labor Relations Review, 9/1956/–.

[17] *United States, Dept. of Labor, Women's Bureau* (ed.): Highlights of women's employment and education. Washington, D.C.: Employment Standards Administration, Women's Bureau 1974.

[18] *Sommers, Dixie; Eck, Alan:* Occupational mobility in the American labor force. In: Monthly Labor Review, –/1977/Jan., pp. 3-19.

[19] Why corporations are on the move. In: Fortune, –/1976/May.

[20] *Rappaport; Rappaport:* The dual career family. See also: They manage both, careers and kids. In: National Observer, –/1977/January 1. (Front page article.)

[21] *Hall, Douglas T.:* A model of coping with role conflict. The role behavior of college educated women. In: Administrative Science Quarterly, 17/1972/4, pp. 471–486.

[22] *Murray, Edwin A.:* The social response process in commercial banks. An empirical investigation. In: The Academy of Management Review, 1/1976/3. See also: *Murray, Edwin A.:* The implementation of social policies in commercial banks. Cambridge, Mass.: Harvard Univ., diss. 1974.

Joyce Hocker Frost

The influence of female and male communication styles on conflict strategies: Problem areas*

"Conflict styles develop for good reasons. *No one style is automatically better than another.*" *Schuetz* discussed bargaining styles in terms of "reasonableness, rationality, and logic," (*Schuetz* 1975) giving a different connotation to these words than usually is assumed. In her viewpoint, everyone's conflict behavior is reasonable *to that person* – the behavior is chosen, consciously or unconsciously, because it makes sense to that person in that situation. Others may disagree about the choice of behavior. "Rationality" then becomes important – a person's conflict behavior is seen as rational not by some outside standard of what constitutes rational behavior such as reliance on formal logic, use of expert evidence and a calm, unemotional approach, but by how well a person's choice of behavior moves him or her toward desired goals given the facts of the persons involved in the conflict, their particular relationship to each other, and the requirements of the situation at that time.

People who can change and adapt are more likely to be effective conflict participants, gaining private and group goals better than people who avoid change. *Hart* and *Burks* (1972) in their article "Rhetorical sensitivity and social interaction" discuss the concept of rhetorical sensitivity – of persons who have skills in goal-directed communication. They give the following five characteristics of persons who are rhetorically sensitive:

1. They are able to alter their roles in response to the behaviors of others and accept their alteration of roles in response to someone else.

2. They avoid stylizing their communication behavior so they are able to adapt.

3. They are able to withstand the pressure and ambiguity of constant adaptation and will develop skills of dealing with different audiences.

4. They are able to monitor talk with others to make it purposive rather than expressive. They speak not so much to "spill their guts" as to solve problems.

* The paper was presented at the 27th Annual Conference of the International Communication Association, Berlin, June 1977. Much of the material was taken from: *Frost,* Joyce Hocker; *Wilmot,* William W.: Interpersonal conflict. Dubuque, Iowa: W.C. Brown 1978. XIV, 182 p.

5. They alter behaviors and carry on adaptation in a rational and orderly way. (*Hart* and *Burks,* 1972)

In other words, effective interpersonal communicators expect change and adapt to change in their communication with others. They avoid getting "stuck" in certain conflict styles.

Gender related conflict differences

In the following section I will explore some of the conflict differences resulting from our socialization as males and females. Individual differences are more important than simple assumptions about sex roles, but I concur with some of the recent research on gender related communication differences. People report that they intuitively notice differences in the way men and women do conflict. For instance, men tend to say that women "get emotional," and women tend to say that men "are overly competitive." In any discussion about conflict styles, we should remember that one sex's *perception* of differences in the opposite sex is just as important as research reporting on specific differences. Self-fulfilling prophecies come into play – men and women choose behaviors in conflict situations partially because they are expected to choose those behaviors. Therefore, we must look not only at relatively objective data giving a picture of what men and women do differently, but at what they *think* they do differently.

In a recent class on conflict management, students were asked to reflect on how conflict was handled in their homes, and to think about how their individual attitudes toward conflict developed. Women overwhelmingly reported the experience of learning to *avoid* conflict. *Bardwick,* for example (1971) has noted that girls are socialized into drastically lower levels of activity in conflict. This was emphasized by some of the responses from the class. One woman reported:

"As a child, I was forbidden to 'talk back.' As a result, I stifled all my replies until I was of sufficient age to walk out and did so. That was fifteen years ago – I have never been back . . . Thus, my strategy has been one of avoidance of a conflict to which I can see no resolution. As I had been raised by my father and stepmother, I scarcely knew my mother. When I was seventeen, I went to live with her. She wanted a mother-daughter relationship to which I could not respond. Legally bound to her, my attempts at confrontation ended in failure. Once again I walked out – this time into marriage. After seven years of marriage and abortive attempts at communication, I again walked out – this time with two children."

Another student reported that she was raised in a gentle, peaceful family where there was little conflict, and "never saw my parents angry with each other, and seldom with us four children." Thus she reported she has been trying to live up to what she now views as an unreal expectation of peace and harmony.

Not only was avoidance the primary tactic used by these women, but they also discussed the inability to sense the feelings that *might* lead to conflict. Another student said:

> "In our home, conflict was avoided or denied at all costs, so I grew up without having the experience of seeing conflicts managed in a satisfactory way, and I felt that conflict was somehow 'bad' and would never be resolved. This experience fitted well with the rewards of being a 'good' girl (compliant), combining to make a pattern for me in which I was not even sensitive to wishes and desires which might lead to conflict."

Thus, the fear of conflict combined with female role stereotyping to produce an avoidance pattern.

Another common pattern remembered by some of the women in the class was the *temper tantrum*. Girls were not punished as severely as boys for exhibiting uncontrollable emotion. This behavior, which seems incongruous for a grown woman, was reported by many women. Pouting, angry crying and screaming is a method women said they sometimes used when they felt that they were in a low power situation. Grown women, feeling a lack of power by little practice in and reinforcement for dealing with conflicts productively, have traditionally been expected to resort to tactics more appropriate for children. In the study, *Dick and Jane as victims* (1973), a review of texts and readers for elementary school children, one of the common patterns for little girls involved in competition or conflict was not only the tantrum, but "giving up!" One frame shows a boy saying to his mother about his sister, who has fallen on her skates, "she's just like a girl – she gives up!"

As we stated earlier, however, both men and women suffer from stereotypic styles used in dealing with conflicts, especially with each other. This example illustrates the boxes both men and women get into in their conflict relationships:

> "A prime example of conflict was my recently ended twenty-nine year marriage. We never raised our voices. I felt I was the keeper of the peace over the years. I always avoided 'scenes.' In the last few years my desire to develop my abilities and make use of them in a part-time job . . . created a conflict situation. At that time belligerent words were exchanged, if not in raised voices. At such times, he would say, 'There's no point in talking about it now; it will only make matters worse.' (His saying *that*

made matters worse!) To proceed to do what I wanted to do against his will was a frightening thing (not because of fear of any physical violence, but because of disapproval.) My former husband became my main 'proving ground' for my newer strategies in conflict. I finally succeeded in standing up to him."

The losses both parties accrued in this conflict are evident. The man was unwilling or afraid to discuss the woman's feeling. The woman was so used to the role of "peacekeeper" for the dyad that she could not change her role without getting out of the relationship altogether. They were caught in a *regressive communication spiral, (Wilmot,* 1975) with no useful strategies for continuing the relationship in spite of the conflict. All the woman could do was repeat the adolescent cycle of rebelling against "father" and walk out.

Just as with women, men also are socialized into standardized approaches to conflicts. When men are asked in our workshops "what women do well in conflict," they typically respond, "women use their emotions to get what they want." In discussion, it becomes clear that men feel that expressing emotions is a powerful tool that women use because men can't "handle it when women cry." Similarly, men describe conflicts in aggressive, power-oriented terms. They often speak of "having it out," "decking the SOB," "not taking any s . . ." Furthermore, men are socialized into believing that the relational training that women receive (learning to attune to feelings and to the relational impacts of conflicts) gives women an "unfair advantage because they know what is going on." As a result, men are prone to push for "airing the issues" and "getting things on the table" in a manner that focuses attention on the content issues as compared to the relationship issues.

Men and women not only learn different overall strategies for doing conflict, such as avoidance, escalation, reduction or maintenance, *they also learn to speak differently. Eakins* and *Eakins* (1977) report that women learn to do more expressive speaking than men. Expressive speech tells about the emotions of the speaker, his or her relationship to the other, and tends to be creative and tangential. Verbal expressiveness is often interpreted, in *Berne's* words (1964) as "stroking," or raising the status of another person, giving help, and providing attention to another person. This verbal stroking can be in the form of asking for opinions, asking for suggestions, for clarification, or of agreeing, reinforcing the statements of others, and complying with what another person wants you to do. Men often learn to depend on these expressions by women, and when they are not forthcoming, they think the woman is acting aggressively.

129

Men, on the other hand, often use task oriented language. A study of mock jury deliberations revealed that while women contributed more positive (stroking) reactions to statements of others and showed more tension release, such as laughing more, men tended to describe the situation and make more suggestions for future action than did the women. They gave more opinions and "orientation talks." Men used more "let's get the job done" talk, while women used more expressions of support and solidarity (*Strodtbeck* and *Mann,* 1956).

Men and women who choose to change their behavior, or who simply never have conformed to these stereotypic expectations, often are thought to be very peculiar. While "men in general" are thought to be good at task orientation, and "women in general" are thought to be good at the socio-emotional orientation of communication in groups, not everyone fits this pattern. Men, for instance, who prefer to listen and support the ideas of women in the group are sometimes thought to be "passive" and withdrawn. Women who actively seek to reach decisions quickly and move the group along are labelled as "aggressive" and pushy.

The following suggestions may help in counseling both men and women who are dissatisfied with their roles in organizations: Hopefully, counseling before the grievance escalates can help eliminate court battles and extreme role dissatisfaction.

1. Clarify your role when appropriate. For instance, you might say, "I have taken a supportive role for whatever the group is trying to come up with for a solution to our conflicts, but I am too involved in this conflict to be comfortable with that role, so I will be speaking up more."

2. Seek feedback when you think you are being ignored. Women often report the feeling that "When I try to get involved in the conflict, it's like a river just flows around me and continues on the other side after I talk." If this happens to you (either sex!) you can ask questions after you finish. You can ask people to respond to your suggestion before they go on. You can assert that you think your statement is important and you don't want it ignored or overlooked.

3. You can point out when someone else is assigning you a role with which you are not comfortable at the time. You might say, for instance, "I get the feeling that you are expecting me to come up with some way out of this hassle. I don't know the way out. I'm as angry and confused as you are. We're going to have to work together."

4. You can simply quit doing some of the communication behaviors with which you are not pleased at the time. Women can conciliate less when they don't feel like conciliating; men can stay quiet when they don't want to or can't think of problem-solving suggestions. Sometimes silence in a conflict situation forces other people with good ideas to express them, instead of depending on the habitual responses of others.

Men and women also react differently to competitive situations. In game-like situations, when the sexes are pitted against each other, women tend to play more cooperatively against men than they do against women. Men play more competitively against women than they do against other men – a strange finding in the light of the usual assumption that men are most aggressive and competitive against each other in sports, for instance. Women compete more against each other than they do against men (*Borgatta* and *Stimson,* 1963). Thus, the introduction of the opposite sex may tone down competitive behavior of women but spark this behavior in men. No wonder, then, that men and women have so much trouble working through conflicts with each other. Women are often startled by the intense competition that men exhibit – which may be more intense than men do with each other. Men may assume that women aren't very competitive – when they are more competitive in single sex groups. Of course, as some note, the fact that this research is done in a competitively structured game may pose some problems, since men may be presumed to be more accustomed to such situations. Practical suggestions coming from these findings, however, might be explored. In work situations where competition is important male managers might do well to initially put women in small groups or single sex groups in the beginning phases of their job orientation. Then the success they have in sales, for instance, might more easily be generalized across mixed sex groups in the future. In noncompetitive situations, women can be rewarded for their supportive and expressive behavior while being encouraged to bring up ideas and be assertive. Men can be rewarded for their task orientation, while they are being asked careful questions about how they are responding emotionally to conflict situations. The sexes can help each other out, building on the strengths of each.

Another pattern of communication behavior that differs according to the sex of the person is *interruption behavior.* Have you had the experience of being told that you interrupt all the time and that you are rude? Or have you felt that you could never get a word in edgewise? People often drive others to distraction because they don't listen, or they blow up when they think they aren't being heard by the other people in the conflict. One person may sulk for days in righteous indignation over the overbearing manner of the other, while the other might assume that he has been considerate, has listened well, and has facilitated the conflict by giving helpful suggestions and keeping things "on the track." Some of these reactions may be tied to sex related differences. *Eakins and Eakins* (1977) discuss interruption patterns of men and women, and point out that men talk more in groups of people, and in part they attain this right to talk more by interrupting women and each other far more than women interrupt men (*Kester,* 1972). Women also tend to let men interrupt – they do not "fight back" for their turns in conversations as much as men do. *Zimmerman and West* (1975) found that in same-sex conversations interruptions were distributed fairly evenly with no differences between men and women. But in male-female conversations, the patterns were different. Ninety-eight to a hundred per cent of the interruptions were carried out by men. The transcripts of the conversations revealed no complaints from the women such as "You keep interrupting me," or "Let me finish."

Men to whom I have reported these results often are astonished, while women indicate that they knew something was happening. This does not assume, of course, that men are inherently rude and that women are polite – but that socialization is different, and people often attribute evil intent to the other side, or assume that the other person had nothing to say. Again, as in role difficulties in groups, people can change their behavior if they want to. The author once entered into a pact with a female colleague on her faculty. They agreed to support each other when the other one was interrupted – to use phrases such as "Wait a minute, I want to hear what she has to say," or "Let her finish, please." After two meetings, several male colleagues remarked upon entering the meeting that they hoped they "weren't going to have to fight the women again," and hoped "You're in a better mood than last time." In one of my classes, two students were role playing a conflict about who should be the next U.S. President, in which the woman frequently interrupted the man. The man, a usually articulate and outspoken member, was so astonished he could not even think of arguments. He said she was "attacking" and "destroying" him. Women who refuse to be interrupted, or who interrupt, will often incur hostility from males. And, men who sincerely try not to interrupt as much as they often have in the past are sometimes accused by girlfriends of "not being interested" or being "distracted." Old patterns die hard!

An important assumption, however, is that interruption patterns can be challenged and changed, and both people (or three, or ten) can gain a sense of respect for other parties by learning to listen carefully and actively. Women feel more confident when they fight back for a turn, thus bearing less hostility toward the male with which they are having a conflict, and men learn to slow down and listen, thus experiencing a higher quality decision made by the group and more satisfaction afterwards. Patterns can change.

Finally, I find that women use more accommodative conflict strategies, while men use competitive or exploitive ones. Men are more comfortable with winning, while women are more comfortable with finding a fair outcome, acceptable to all. Neither of these strategies is inherently "good." Sometimes the structure of a conflict is set up for winning and losing, and sometimes the structure is cooperative. The problem occurs when men and women get stuck in a role and cannot change when it is appropriate to change. For instance, in a conflict with parents and a teenage child over whether the child should drop out of school, the mother may find herself wanting everyone to be happy, when the hard reality is that they are, at the moment, locked into a win (stay in school) – lose (the child leaves school) setup. Rather than accommodation, a better choice would be to work to redefine the decision. Men may find themselves saying after a conflict over money with their wife, "I got her to see my point of view," when they are locked into an interdependent system in which the wife can subvert any system that she does not agree with. He would have been better off to drop the self-advantage approach and work toward a mutually accommodative solution.

We might all encourage men and women to explore their conflict roles, ask whether they are satisfied with them, and consider changing their habitual patterns when such change is appropriate. Friends, family and co-workers can be an invaluable source of feedback for persons who are curious about their conflict styles.

In conclusion, several guides are offered for determining if the conflict rituals operating in relationships are productive or destructive. When persons seek advice from EEO officers, discuss with co-workers whether to try to implement change, or perhaps when they work on conflicts in organizationally sponsored training sessions, these suggestions will be useful for beginning the process of looking at ongoing, ritualistic conflicts involving men and women.

1. Are the parties stuck in a conflict style that seems to continue regardless of their efforts to change it? Often, destructive conflict can be identified when the participants have a feeling of being "out of control" of the relationship.

When both parties say that they want to improve the relationship, yet their individual styles interlock in such a way that they both end up being miserable and unhappy, then the relationship rituals are not working for them. When the ritual gets so ingrained that the parties cannot have the freedom to change it (and want to), then the conflicts are likely to not be productive.

2. Are personal goals accomplished in the conflicts? If one of the parties finds that her or his goals are rarely accomplished, perhaps the relationship has been frozen in ways that are not productive. If the secretary finds that every time her boss curses at her, she backs down and withdraws on the issue, then she loses her ability to influence those decisions. Perpetually feeling powerless and helpless is a sign that your relationship rituals are not productive for you.

3. Do you find yourself trying to injure or wanting to harm the other person? If you find that in important relationships you come away from conflicts with a desire to "get" the other person, such a feeling can be a clue that somehow the relationship rituals have not been productive. The original goals in most conflicts are not to injure the other person – those vengeful feelings arise from feeling blocked from accomplishing your initial goals. For instance, if the participant in a small group wants to "clobber the leader over the head to make him shut-up" that is a sign that the leader's talkativeness is blocking some important goals of the participant. It may be that the self-esteem of the participant is suffering because he wants to make more contributions to the group and the leader preempts him. In any event, hostile feelings toward another are a sign that the rituals you have worked out for the relationship are not working for you.

The closer relationships can operate to fulfill the goals of the parties involved, the more healthy they will be. Destructive conflicts can be pinpointed by observing the relational blockages and using their existence as a guide to the health of the relationship. Both individuals and relationships can be characterized as having styles – the characteristic modes that emerge during the doing of conflict.

A good reason for determining your individual and relationship styles in conflict situations is that one comes to realize that behavior is *stylistic,* that it is learned instead of inherent (since people aren't born with conflict styles) and that *it can change.*

References

Alberti, Robert E.; Emmons, Michael L.: Your perfect right. A guide to assertive behavior. 2nd ed. San Luis Obispo, Calif: Impact Press 1974. 118 p.

Altman, Irwin; Taylor, Dalmas A.: Social penetration. The development of interpersonal relationships. New York: Holt, Rinehart and Winston 1973. XX, 212 p.

Bach, George R.; Wyden, Peter: The intimate enemy. How to fight fair in love and marriage. New York: Avon Co. 1968. 384 p.

Bardwick, Judith M.: Psychology of women. A study of bio-cultural conflicts. New York: Harper and Row. 1971. VII, 242 p.

Berne, Eric: Games people play. The psychology of human relationships. New York: Grove Press 1964. 192 p.

Blake, Robert Rogers; Mouton, Jane S.: The managerial grid. Key orientations for achieving production through people. Houston. Tex.: Gulf Publishing Co. 1964. XII, 340 p.

Borgatta, E.F.; Stimson, J.: Sex differences in interaction characteristics. In: Journal of Social Psychology, 60/1963/–, pp. 89 – 100.

Eakins, Barbara Westbrook; Eakins, R. Gene: Female-male communication. Boston: Houghton-Mifflin 1977.

Ellis, Don; Fisher, B. Aubrey: Phases of conflict in small group development. A Markow analysis. In: Human Communication Research, 1/1973/–, pp. 195 – 212.

Frost, Joyce Hocker; Wilmot, William W.: Interpersonal conflict. Dubuque, Iowa: W.C. Brown 1978, XIV, 182 p.

Glick, Bruce; Gross, Steven: Marital interaction and marital conflict. A critical evaluation of current research strategies. In: Journal of Marriage and the Family, 317/1975/–, pp. 505 – 512.

Hall, Jay: Conflict management survey. A survey of one's characteristic reaction to and handling of conflicts between himself and others. Conroe, Tex.: Teleometrics International 1969.

Harré, R.: Some remarks on 'rule' as a scientific concept. In: Mischel, Theodore (ed.): Understanding other persons. Oxford: Basil Blackwell 1974.

Harré, Romano; Secord, P.F.: The explanation of social behavior. Totowa, N.J.: Littlefield, Adams and Co. 1973. VI, 327 p.

Hart, Roderick P.; Burks, Don M.: Rhetorical sensitivity and social interaction. In: Speech Monographs, 39/1972/June.

Jamieson, D.; Thomas, K.: Power and conflict in the student-teacher relationship. In: Journal of Applied Behavioral Science, 10/1974/–, pp. 321 – 336.

Kester, Judy. Report in: Parade Magazine, –/1972/Mai 7.

Kilmann, Ralph; Thomas, Kenneth: Interpersonal conflict-handling behavior as reflections of Jungian personality dimensions. In: Psychological Reports, 37/1975/–, pp. 971 – 980.

Kilmann, Ralph; Thomas, Kenneth: Developing a forced-choice measure of conflict-handling behavior. The 'mode' instrument. In: Educational and Psychological Measurement, 37/1977/–, pp. 309 – 325

Lawrence, P.R.; Lorsch, J.W.: Differentiation and integration in complex organization. In: Administrative Science Quarterly, 12/1967/–, pp. 1 – 47.

Lederer, William J.; Jackson, Don D.: Mirages of marriage. New York: Norton 1968. 473 p.

Raush, Herold L. (coll.); *Barry, W.A.* (coll.); *Hertel, R.K.* (coll.) et al.: Communication, conflict and marriage. San Francisco: Jossey Bass 1974. XII, 250 p.

Rodgers, L. Edna; Farace, Richard: Analysis of relational communication in dyads. In: Human Communication Research, 1/1975/–, pp. 222 – 239.

Ruble, T.L.; Thomas, Kenneth: Support for a two dimensional model of conflict behavior. In: Organizational Behavior and Human Performance, 16/1976/–, pp. 143 – 155.

Schuetz, Janice E.: A contingent model of argumentation based on a game theory paradigm. Boulder, Colo., Univ. of Colorado, diss. 1975.

Strodbeck, Fred; Mann, Richard: Sex role differentiation in jury deliberations. In: Sociometry, 19/1956/March, pp. 3 – 11.

Tedeschi, James T.; Schlenker, Barry R.; Bonoma, Thomas V.: Conflict, power and games. The experimental study of interpersonal relations. Chicago: Aldine 1973. X, 270 p.

Thomas, Kenneth; Kilmann, Ralph: The social desirability variable in organizational research. In: Academy of Management Journal, 41/1975/–, pp. 413 – 420.

Thomas, Kenneth; Kilmann, Ralph: Some properties of existing conflict behavior instruments. Los Angeles, Calif.: Univ. of California, Graduate School of Management 1973.

Valentine, Kristen; Fisher, B. Aubrey: An interaction analysis of verbal innovative deviance in small groups. In: Speech Monographs, 41/1974/–, pp. 413 – 420.

Villard, Kenneth; Whipple, Leland J.: Beginnings in relational communications. New York: Wiley 1976. XI, 275 p.

Wilmot, William W.: Dyadic communication. A transactional perspective. Reading, Mass.: Addison-Wesley 1975. XV, 196 p.

Zimmerman, Don H.; West, Candaca: Sex roles, interruptions and silence in conversation. In: Thorne, Barrie (ed.) et al.: Language and sex. Difference and dominance. Rowley, Mass.: Newbury House 1975.

Authors

Aimee *Dorr,* M.A., Ph. D., Associate Professor in the Annenberg School of Communications at the University of Southern California, Los Angeles; from 1972–1978 Assistant and then Associate Professor in the Center for Research in Children's Television, Laboratory of Human Development, Harvard University Graduate School of Education; from 1967–1972 Assistant Professor in the Department of Communications at Stanford University.

Joyce Hocker *Frost,* Ph.D., Associate Professor of Interpersonal Communication, University of Montana, Missoula. Co-author of Interpersonal conflict (1978). Formerly Assistant Professor, Department of Communication, University of Colorado. Currently a post-doctoral student in clinical psychology, University of Montana, with special training in family therapy.

Marianne *Grewe-Partsch,* Dr. jur., responsible for the field of putting research results into practice at the Internationales Zentralinstitut für das Jugend- und Bildungsfernsehen, Munich; responsible editor of the journal Fernsehen und Bildung, from 1943 to 1952 publishing director, from 1957 to 1961 staff member at the Pädagogische Arbeitsstelle des Deutschen Volkshochschulverbandes, from 1961 to 1974 Department Director at Hessischer Rundfunk, Frankfurt/M.

Lois Wladis *Hoffman,* Ph. D., developmental psychologist, Professor of Psychology at the University of Michigan, Ann Arbor. Author/editor of Review of child development research, volumes 1 and 2 (1964; 1965); The employed mother in America (1963); Working mothers (1974); Women and achievement (1975) and contributor of many articles to professional journals in psychology.

Mariann *Jelinek,* Ph.D., D.B.A., since 1976 Assistant Professor of Business Administration at the Amos Tuck School, Dartmouth College, Hanover; from 1975–1976 Instructor, Worcester Polytechnic Institute.

Gerald S. *Lesser,* Ph. D., Bigelow Professor of Education and Developmental Psychology and Director of the Center for Research in Children's Television, Laboratory of Human Development, Harvard University Graduate School of Education; from 1956–1963 Associate Professor of Education at Hunter College, City University of New York; from 1954–1956, Assistant Professor of Education and Psychology at Adelphi College.

Gertrude Joch *Robinson,* M.A., Ph.D., Associate Professor of Sociology and Associate Director of the Interdisciplinary Communications Program at McGill University in Montreal. She teaches courses in mass communication, media theory, as well as popular culture and is presently working on a Ministère de Communication (Québec) financed study comparing French and English Canadian press coverage of world events.

Honors and awards include Phi Beta Kappa and Kappa Tau Alpha, as well as two major grants, one from the Yugoslav Government for doctoral research in Belgrade during 1964 and the other from the American Association of University Women for a 1968 study of the changing role of the writer under socialism.

Hertha *Sturm,* Dr. phil., Dipl. Psych., Professor of the Science of Communication at the University of Munich, Scientific Director of the Internationales Zentralinstitut für das Jugend- und Bildungsfernsehen, Munich; from 1953 to 1963 Head of the Radio Program for Schools and Young People of the Südwestfunk; from 1963 to 1968 Head of the Department for Educational Programs of the Zweites Deutsches Fernsehen; 1967 Dr. phil. habil. from the University of Freiburg/Br.; from 1968 to 1974 Professor of Psychology at the University of Freiburg/Br.

Ellen A. *Wartella,* Ph.D., Research Assistant Professor, Institute of Communications Research, University of Illinois at Urbana-Champaign; from 1976 to 1979 Assistant Professor, Department of Communications, Ohio State University; from 1971 to 1976 Research Assistant and Research Associate, Communication Research Division, School of Journalism and Mass Communication, University of Minnesota; NDEA Fellow, University of Minnesota.

School Radio in Europe

A documentation
with contributions given at the
European School Radio Conference,
Munich 1977

Edited by
Internationales Zentralinstitut für
das Jugend- und Bildungsfernsehen
(IZI)
1979. 198 p. DM 28.—.
(Communication Research and
Broadcasting No. 1)
ISBN 3-598-20200-8

This documentation informs about
the structure and objectives of 41
school radio departments in 20
European countries. The following
main subjects are dealt with:
— The situation of school radio in
  Europe
— Issues in perception and attention in relation to the reception
  of radio broadcasts
— Foreign language teaching and
  school radio
— Music education in school radio
— What is the future of school
  radio?
The publication is also available in
German. There is also a Spanish edi-
tion which can be ordered directly
from: Internationales Zentralinstitut für das Jugend- und Bildungs-
fernsehen, Rundfunkplatz 1, 8000
München 2.

Effects and Functions of Television: Children and Adolescents

A bibliography of selected research
literature 1970—1978

Compiled by
Manfred Meyer and Ursula Nissen

1979. 172 p. DM 24.—.
(Communication Research and
Broadcasting No. 2)
ISBN 3-598-20201-6

This research bibliography concen-
trates on the use of television and
its varying functions for children
and adolescents, and on the effects
of television programmes on their
personality development and socialization. It contains references to
publications in English, French and
German, with a focus on European
research work. Contents include:
mass communication research: in-
troductions, readers, reviews; studies
on the uses and functions of television and other media; studies on
the effects of television violence on
social behaviour; formative and
summative research on TV series
for children; studies on the effects
of television advertising; etc.

K·G·Saur München · New York · London · Paris

K·G·Saur Verlag KG · Postfach 71 10 09 · 8000 München 71 · Tel. (0 89) 79 89 01 · Telex 05 212 067 saur d